The Practical Guide to

CLASSROOM LITERACY ASSESSMENT

The Practical Guide to

CLASSROOM
LITERACY
ASSESSMENT

Diane Barone
Joan M. Taylor

CORWIN PRESS
A SAGE Publications Company
Thousand Oaks, CA 91320

For information:

Corwin Press
A Sage Publications Company
2455 Teller Road
Thousand Oaks, California 91320
www.corwinpress.com

Sage Publications Ltd.
1 Oliver's Yard
55 City Road
London, EC1Y 1SP
United Kingdom

Sage Publications India Pvt. Ltd.
B-42, Panchsheel Enclave
Post Box 4109
New Delhi 110 017 India

Printed in the United States of America

Library of Congress Cataloging-in-Publication Data

Barone, Diane
The practical guide to classroom literacy assessment/Diane Barone and Joan M. Taylor.
    p. cm.
Includes bibliographical references and index.
ISBN 1-4129-3913-5 or 978-1-4129-3913-3 (cloth)
ISBN 1-4129-3914-3 or 978-1-4129-3914-0 (pbk.)
  1. Language arts (Elementary)–Evaluation. 2. Reading (Elementary)–Evaluation.
3. Educational tests and measurements. I. Taylor, Joan. II. Tittle.
LB1576.B315 2007
372.6—dc22   2006018260

This book is printed on acid-free paper.

07   08   09   10   10 9 8 7 6 5 4 3 2 1

Acquisitions Editor:	Jean Ward
Editorial Assistant:	Jordan Barbakow
Production Editor:	Beth A. Bernstein
Copy Editor:	Carol Anne Peschke
Typesetter:	C&M Digitals (P) Ltd.
Proofreader:	Anna Rogers
Indexer:	Rick Hurd
Cover Designer:	Rose Storey
Graphic Designer:	Lisa Riley

Contents

Acknowledgments

Corwin Press gratefully acknowledges the contributions of the following reviewers:

Amy Huether
SD READS Literacy Coach
Black Hills Special Services Cooperative
New Underwood, SD

Joan Irwin
Professional Development Consultant
Newark, DE

Nancy McDonough
Second-Grade Teacher
Walter Stillman School
Tenafly, NJ

Vickie McCullah
Reading First Coach
Howe Public School
Howe, OK

Carol K. Weber
GT/Enrichment Resource Teacher and Reading Specialist
Cherry Creek Schools
Aurora, CO

Ken Goodwin
Elementary School Principal
P.S. DuPont Elementary/Brandywine School District
Wilmington, DE

About the Authors

 **Diane Barone** is a professor of literacy studies at the University of Nevada, Reno. In her role at the university, she teaches courses in early literacy, diversity and literacy, and qualitative research. Her research interests center on young children, especially in high-poverty schools, and how they develop in literacy. Her most current study followed 16 children from kindergarten through Grade 6 to document their literacy growth.

She has been an editor of *Reading Research Quarterly* and has written numerous articles, book chapters, and books. Some of her recent books include *Reading First in the Classroom* with Joan M. Taylor and Darrin Hardman, *Literacy and Young Children: Research-Based Practices* with Lesley Morrow, *Teaching Early Literacy: Development, Assessment, and Instruction* with Marla Mallette and Shelley Xu, and *The National Board Certification Handbook*. She is also principal investigator for Reading First in Nevada.

 **Joan M. Taylor** is a teacher-consultant who works with teachers and students in Title I schools in the Reno-Sparks area of northern Nevada. She recently completed a dissertation on *A History of Written Composition Instruction in U.S. Elementary Schools*. In addition to historical and current perspectives on writing instruction, her research interests are focused on exploring teachers' stories on learning and teaching.

She has been a longtime middle school teacher in Washoe County Schools. She is also a Nevada State Networks Writing Project codirector, and in the past several years she has authored a number of federally funded state literacy grants from the U.S. Department of Education totaling approximately $53 million. These include the Nevada Reading Excellence Act and Nevada Reading First grants.

Introduction

Assessments and evaluation have always existed in some form in public schooling in the United States. From the earliest days of colonial America, when selectmen visited homes to make sure parents were complying with statutes mandating that they teach their children to read, to current accountability testing procedures at national and state levels, we as a people have demonstrated a commitment to the future of our nation by assessing our efforts to educate future generations. However, not until recently have national initiatives focused so closely on assessment results to ensure that all students across socioeconomic levels, all races and ethnic groups, with any disabilities, demonstrate similarly high academic literacy proficiencies.

The Practical Guide to Classroom Literacy Assessment provides information about testing content and procedures that we believe is important for teachers, administrators, parents, and students. All assessments—national, state, district, and classroom based—have some similarities in their design and focus. All are directed at student achievement, whether it is to track progress of individual students or student cohorts, to determine the best allocation of resources, to evaluate materials and programs, or to refer individual students for specialized instruction. In addition, all assessments come with predetermined sets of criteria for evaluation, and all can be viewed from multiple perspectives. We owe it to our students to help them with this newest of literacies, assessment literacy, to deal with the inevitable testing they will experience.

One important way to deal with these assessments is to help students learn to anticipate what test items will be asked. Students who can look at a math illustration or a social studies graph and already begin to think about what kinds of questions will accompany the pictorial often are at an advantage over those who are still trying to figure out what the drawing represents. By the same token, the main reason smart students miss problems they should have aced is that they anticipate to the point of answering the wrong question; that is, the one that immediately came to mind instead of the one actually being asked. Good readers and listeners use background knowledge to predict and ask questions before and as they read or listen and reflect, and they alter their questions and predictions as they read and contemplate the text's meaning. Good test takers do, too.

In this book, we hope to give teachers and their students some expectations for testing items and ways to help students anticipate the types of questions they will be asked. Through assessments in multiple formats and as part of regular instructional practice, thoughtfully planned instructional activities can be adapted to the needs of students who have not learned from instruction designed to meet the needs of most students. By involving students in these multiple assessments of their own learning, we can assist them in setting goals and monitoring their own progress as a part of their total instructional plan.

Testing tools and instruments should be part of total evaluation feedback; that is, the beginning of evaluation, not the end. We offer rubrics and checklists in the following chapters as a means to an end, not an end in themselves. They offer a basis for student-teacher discussions that guide future instruction and are framed to help students think about ways they can improve performance rather than a means of defining their lack of proficiency.

The focus of this book is literacy assessments—not just the anticipated reading tests but also assessments designed to measure writing, listening, speaking, and viewing and their implications for classroom instruction and student learning. We know that teachers will value the information presented here and use it to meet the strengths and needs of their students through assessments that guide instruction and enhance student learning. We anticipate that this information will also provide a basis for collegial discussions on assessments and instruction and informative parent conferences on student progress.

Assessments With a Focus on Learning

Purposes and Promises

When you hear the word test, what is your immediate response?

    a. I feel sick.

    b. I feel angry.

    c. I feel stupid.

    d. I feel nervous.

Are you looking for the *all of the above* choice in these selected responses? If so, you are not alone. Many people suffer from test anxiety. However, some people are anxious, while others appear to revel in the challenge of matching wits with test items. We have experienced the range of emotions both as students and as teachers of students facing high- and low-stakes tests. Perhaps the first step in relieving test anxiety is being able to understand some of the reasons for assessing literacy.

THE HISTORICAL ROOT OF THE MATTER

True or false? With the advent of the standards movement, testing has become a new and important priority for teachers and students.

We hope you chose *false* on this one. Although widespread public attention to testing results has captured the public's interest through recent government policies and media coverage, taking tests is not a new American trend. If we were to time-travel back to the early nineteenth-century United States, we would find school board members arriving in classrooms, sometimes unannounced and sometimes according to plan, and delivering oral examinations to cross-graded classes full of students. Our teacher colleagues from the past stood to one side, watching and listening hopefully for demonstrations of their students' mastered skills. Although it may not have felt the same as reading standardized test reports today, the hopeful anticipation of a good showing and the feelings of disappointment at failure surely must have been similar. Test equity issues were also apparent back then. School board members sometimes were accused of playing favorites by saving the most difficult questions for the children of rivals and the simplest test items for the children of friends and business associates.

Also in the nineteenth century, schools usually were expected to offer exhibitions of work accomplished by pupils. In his account of country schools in the nineteenth-century United States, Clifton Johnson described "examination day," when the schoolroom was cleaned and the students came attired in their "Sunday-go-to-meetin's" for a community gathering to showcase student work. "Scholars were called out to recite such things as they knew best, and possibly to speak a few pieces and read compositions" (1907, p. 112).

In 1904, the National Education Association appointed a committee to study the use of tests in classifying children and determining their progress. Early scientific reading assessments included gathering student data on eye movements, visual perceptions, reading speed, lip movements during silent reading, and automatic word recognition for reading ahead in oral reading. Mechanical devices called tachistoscopes allowed readers to view only certain letters, words, or phrases as researchers tracked eye movements and questioned participants on the retelling of words or selected texts. Comprehension tests usually required subjects to recall information from a first or second reading. Edmund Huey, noted researcher at the beginning of the twentieth century, attempted to link assessment and research information to instruction by recommending font types and lines per page (Venezky, 1984).

Historian Nila Smith (1934/1970) describes a rapid increase in scientific investigations in reading coinciding with the advent of standardized tests in the 1920s. They became common around the country in the 1920s and 1930s, with multiple-choice item responses providing collective and individual information on students' literacy proficiencies. This information often was connected with grade placement and promotion and with achievement comparisons from school to school.

In their quest to provide individualized instruction, progressive educators in the years between the two world wars sought testing as a diagnostic tool for instructional grouping and as a way to identify learning disabilities. With the introduction of the Stanford Achievement Battery assessments during this time, simultaneous assessment of multiple school subjects was possible. The tests held promise for the entire education community on the grounds that "they are convenient, interesting, take less time to use, and bring into light particular difficulties which the pupils have encountered and which are a bar to their progress" (Almack & Lang, 1925, p. 148). Other educators during this time proclaimed the growth of measurement and experimentation as "one of the marvels of the age" (Caldwell & Courtis, 1925/1971, p. 108).

Concurrently, writing assessments also were receiving greater attention in measuring students' literacy progress. In the early 1900s, Edward L. Thorndike and Milo Hillegas assembled a series of writing examples against which student samples could be measured, compared, and scaled. These scaling systems of sample compositions were later reinvented, replicated, and improved upon by numerous research studies. Some provided graded samples for mixed types of writing, some only offered narrative forms, and others just evaluated letter-writing samples. Several educators in the first quarter of the twentieth century suggested analytically measuring structure, content or thought, and mechanics as separate features, thus anticipating the analytic trait scoring process that later became a popular diagnostic tool for writing teachers (Taylor, 2005).

Although the use of testing in composition was increasing during this time, classroom teachers probably were not greatly influenced by the scaling system trend until the late twentieth century. The time necessary for training and scoring and the additional burden of not only correcting but also comparing student papers made it inefficient for busy educators. However, the foundation was established for future standardized writing assessment practices and concerns. The recurring themes of validity and reliability, objectivity and standardization, scientific solutions, and efficiency models as the means of improving student learning increased in visibility and importance throughout the century and into the next.

With the educational focus on accountability beginning in the 1970s, increased reliance on tests designed to determine instructional choices and funding allocations made large-scale assessments more prevalent and more important in education decision making. Today, large-scale, external assessments measure students for grade promotion, high school graduation, and college admittance and also rank students, teachers, schools, districts, and even states in terms of educational effectiveness and eligibility for federal funding. Other, small-scale assessments used at the school or classroom level provide diagnostic information for instructional decisions and individual assistance.

WHICH LITERACIES?

Please take the quiz on the next page. The definitions are listed in the same row as the dates given. They demonstrate the difficulty in identifying a single definition for literacy today and also the ways in which it has evolved in the last half century. *The Literacy Dictionary* (Harris & Hodges, 1995) lists no less than 38 representative examples of literacy definitions in use today, many of them in connection with competence in specialized fields of knowledge.

Matching

Draw a line connecting items in the left column with the year they were cited by UNESCO in the right column.

The term *literacy* means		
1. The ability of a person who can, with understanding, both read and write a short simple statement on his or her everyday life	a.	1951
2. A continuum of skills including both reading and writing, applied in a social context	b.	1957
3. The possession by an individual of the essential knowledge and skills which enable him or her to engage in all those activities required for effective functioning in his or her group and community and whose attainments in reading, writing, and arithmetic make it possible for him or her to use these skills toward his or her own and the community's development	c.	1962
4. The ability of a person to engage in all those activities in which literacy is required for effective functioning in his group and community and also for enabling him to continue to use reading, writing, and calculation for his own and community's development	d.	1978

NOTE: Based on *The Literacy Dictionary: The Vocabulary of Reading and Writing* (pp. 140–141), edited by T. L. Harris and R. E. Hodges, 1995, Newark, DE: International Reading Association.

The recent national standards documents, as guided by professional organizations, have also suggested contexts in which literacy might be newly defined to assess student knowledge and skills. For example, the National Council of Teachers of Mathematics has noted a shift toward speaking and listening skills and an emphasis on oral and written discourse within mathematics instruction. They describe these processes as a means of helping students to solve problems and to clarify and justify ideas through the use of oral language (National Council of Teachers of Mathematics, 1991).

The National Science Teachers Association has also made spoken and written communications a priority in helping students become active learners. They discuss the means by which teachers can orchestrate discourse in learning communities. Students are asked to explain, clarify, and critically examine and assess their written work (National Research Council, 1996).

The *Curriculum Standards for Social Studies* include reading, writing, and thinking skills as well as abilities to obtain, organize, and deliver information as critical elements of social studies instruction. Essential components of the standards include skills and strategies in acquiring information and manipulating data through reading. Students are also encouraged to develop and present policies, arguments, and stories through instruction and practice in writing (National Council for the Social Studies, 1994).

The national standards document prepared by the International Reading Association and the National Council of Teachers of English, titled *Standards for the English Language Arts,* denotes literacy as spoken, written, and visual language. Spoken language includes listening and speaking skills, written language includes reading and writing skills, and visual language includes two- and three-dimensional texts of a graphic nature that are not text based, such as pictures, concept maps, flowcharts, and video presentations (International Reading Association and National Council of Teachers of English, 1996). It is in these three literacy areas—spoken, written, and visual language—that we will discuss assessments.

AUDIENCES AND TYPES OF ASSESSMENTS

Fill in the blanks:

> *The most important audiences for assessment results are ____, ____, ____, ____, and ____.*

Audiences

Teachers routinely assess student performance to assist in the grading process and to inform students and their parents about progress and effort. Results become an integral part of instruction that informs and guides decisions for individual students and for the class as a whole as teachers determine what students already know and are able to do so they can base instruction on prior knowledge and understanding.

Large-scale and small-scale assessments are really about finding and analyzing patterns of responses to indicate content and process mastery in subject areas. Certainly, teachers and parents are interested in assessment results to identify patterns of students' strengths and weaknesses and to assist student learning. Multiple types of formal and informal assessments, administered regularly, can provide the teacher, the students, and the students' families with accurate and valid information on progress to assist in meeting individual learning needs. To be valid, the assessment must be adequately aligned to the content that is being taught and tested, and it must be useful in making decisions about instruction.

Administrative educators and policymakers are also interested in using assessment results to determine the effectiveness of particular instructional strategies and programs. The data derived from assessments inform decision making and communicate to the general public how effectively an educational system is performing as a whole.

If you filled in the blanks at the beginning of this section with *students, teachers, parents, administrators,* and *policymakers* (presented in any order), you are correct. All these audiences have a vested interest in assessment data and use it to make important educational decisions.

Types

A single test does not provide enough information to support accurate decisions on instruction or progress. A number of reliable assessments must be administered over an extended period of time to provide enough data to make informed judgments on student progress. Reliable assessments consistently correspond to what a test is attempting to measure. This means that scores obtained on one day can be expected to provide comparable data when administered under the same conditions at a later time. This will offer consistent information on students' tendencies to respond in certain ways on the tests.

Educational assessments range from quick checks with teacher signals to see whether everyone understands a concept or agrees with a statement or answer, to individual assessments based on a selection of best student work, to standardized, nationally normed tests. All assessment tools have characteristic strengths and weaknesses. Balancing the effort of preparation, administration, and data analysis of an assessment and the usefulness of its results is a challenge to both test designers and educators.

Formal assessments are especially useful to policymakers and educational administrators for determining trends in student achievement. Norm-referenced tests are developed and administered under standardized conditions and then transformed into scores to reflect a normal curve or bell-shaped distribution around an average. They are then reported in various types of statistical formats to compare groups of students and to provide information on an individual's standing within the assessed population. Conversely, criterion-referenced tests focus on targeted curriculum and assess student proficiency with established criteria based on specific content objectives. Rather than providing results as a basis for comparison with other students, these tests are directed at individual students' particular instructional strengths and needs.

Informal assessments provide important information on processes and learning that cannot be measured in more formal situations. Observations, for example, can determine whether children are altering their behaviors depending on situations and their perceptions based on received information. They are particularly useful in determining whether students are exercising a wide range of strategies as they read, write, speak, and listen. Anecdotal records are another way teachers can document student performance in instructional situations and settings. Parents often rely on weekly or monthly progress reports to keep them informed on curriculum and teachers' assessments and expectations for their children's academic and social progress. These informal assessments are part of good instructional practices and occur on a consistent basis, with teachers usually focusing on a few students each day.

Although true-false, multiple-choice, matching, short-answer, and essay questions are the most common methods used in designing classroom-based assessments, other means by which teachers may assess student progress in an ongoing manner, such as interviews, observations, questioning, discussions, and a variety of visual samples of student work, are equally important.

TIMING OF TESTS

Some reading assessments are aimed specifically at early identification of reading difficulties for immediate instructional interventions. Screening and diagnosis assessments are designed to evaluate student learning needs before instruction. Formative and summative assessments are used during and after instruction to target student populations and determine the effectiveness of the instruction designed to assist them.

Screening measures are used to find which students are at risk for reading difficulty, based on phonemic awareness and early exposure to literacy models. This is the first step in providing additional appropriate instructional strategies to ensure student success in grade-level reading outcomes. In later grades, surveys or preassessments can determine the range of knowledge and abilities in certain areas before instruction and can guide the breadth and depth of needed lessons.

Diagnostic assessments offer more precise information about the need for instruction in specific areas. For example, if a screening test indicates a student's lack of comprehension, a diagnostic assessment might pinpoint the vocabulary words that are limiting understanding of the text. Both standardized and teacher-designed assessments offer practical guidance to help teachers make instructional decisions and offer student support based on information obtained in diagnostic tests.

Formative assessments, both commercially prepared and teacher created, offer information on students' incremental progression, on a monthly, bimonthly, or quarterly schedule. They can take the form of end-of-unit tests, standardized criterion-referenced tests, or teacher-designed tests directly related to content and skills studied. The information generally is reported as progress reports, report cards, spreadsheet data, or part of a narrative. These assessments can identify students in need of additional assistance and can also evaluate different forms of intervention and instruction so that students can receive additional or different forms of instruction that best meet their needs.

Summative assessments generally are provided as a postinstructional assessment. They are designed to evaluate the effectiveness of a literacy program or individual competence mastery at the end of an instructional period to identify areas that need additional attention. They are often reported as individual student grades or in data tables, as in the case of commercially produced and scored tests. Experiences that lead to those summative outcomes also are important and must be described in the summative report.

Through the use of multiple assessments—screening, diagnostic, formative, and summative—a totally integrated evaluation system can provide important information on literacy to determine the next instructional steps for groups of students and for individual students as well. Teachers and schools need to develop a meaningful framework around which assessment collection is organized.

REASONS FOR ASSESSMENTS

Essay: There are a variety of reasons why students are assessed on their literacy skills and knowledge during their academic careers. Explain several reasons for assessments based on each of the language arts areas.

Reasons for Writing Assessments

Charles Schultz, noted creator of *Peanuts* cartoons, sometimes portrays his comic strip characters in situations dealing with writing. One of our favorites depicts a soliloquy by Peppermint Patty as she deals with a test. She laments the substitution of an essay item for one in multiple-choice format and mutters, "I hate when you have to know what you're writing about." This reason is one of the most important ones cited by teachers and test writers who prefer constructed response formats that require students to write extended answers to test questions. Students in this situation have the opportunity to demonstrate what they know rather than what they are able to guess from selected responses.

Writing assessments vary in format and purpose. Some are used to measure students' proficiency with writing tasks, and others are used to determine content knowledge and skills from other areas of the curriculum through the use of writing. Both use written communication skills to determine student knowledge and proficiency.

Objective measures used to evaluate writing skills may be presented in multiple-choice formats, usually with four or five choices. Students are directed to select from among several provided responses to determine the correct punctuation or grammar usage, to select or omit relevant or irrelevant sentences, to manipulate sentence structures, or to reorganize a piece of written text by sequencing the order of provided sentences.

Direct writing assessments are performance based and require students to write in response to an assigned topic or prompt during a specified period of time. These are often called "on-demand" writing tasks. Both on-demand formative assessments, used for diagnostic and instructional purposes, and on-demand summative assessments, used for accountability measurements in writing instruction, generally use holistic or analytic trait-scoring formats. They provide criteria, defined by rubrics that include information for students, teachers, parents, and administrators, to understand achievement levels. They also may include anchor paper samples that provide examples of each level of scoring. More information on these processes is included in Chapter 2.

The writing conference is an additional means of assessment designed to evaluate and support students' progress in writing. Teachers use these opportunities to guide students individually or in small groups through oral discussion about content, style, organization, and editing issues. They can include specialized mini-lessons that target specific needs for each student.

Portfolio collections of student writing are another way of assessing student writing efforts. In addition to being able to document growth over time, they provide opportunities for self-assessments and collaborative assessments between the student and other audiences, including the teacher, peers, and parents. More information on this type of assessment is included in Chapter 5.

Writing assessments used to evaluate achievement in content areas offer questions that are designed to assess the idea development of the response, based on expected standards of content knowledge and skills rather than the process of writing. In these cases, writing itself is not the focus of the evaluation but rather the tool being used to facilitate the assessment. Few would disagree that there is an advantage in being able to use a tool correctly to complete a task with ease and quality. Therefore, the importance of proficient writing skills, though secondary to the primary focus of the assessment, is still essential to performing well on these types of tests.

Reasons for Reading Assessments

Reading assessments are administered before, during, and after reading to guide instruction and learning. Prereading comprehension tests determine background knowledge and can provide motivation for reading. Assessments administered during reading can monitor for potential confusions and misconceptions and can also help students construct their own meanings from text. In book clubs and literature circles, students often provide discussion questions that lead the group in exploring the meanings and writing techniques used by the author. Small group discussions are a way to evaluate student understanding of writing techniques used by authors to connect readers or listeners with content.

In addition, reading assessments allow teachers and parents to understand which strategies and skills students are using and in which they need more instruction and practice. They can also help determine appropriate reading materials at an independent reading level. Current reading assessments determine the ability to recognize and decode words and to demonstrate comprehension of ideas presented in the text. The earliest reading assessments are designed to provide information on student performance that will influence informed instruction and allow intervention measures if needed. Core areas for primary-grade reading assessments include phonemic awareness, phonics, spelling, fluency, vocabulary, and a variety of comprehension skills and strategies, as well as motivation to engage in independent reading practice.

Phonological awareness—that is, the understanding of the component sounds of words in learning to read and spell—is an important area around which beginning reading assessments are centered. Phonemic awareness assessments deal with sound comparisons, phoneme segmentation, and phoneme blending. Phonics assessments explore the sound-symbol relationships used to derive pronunciation of words. They are generally assessed individually through oral and written subtests that determine mastery of the alphabet, letter sounds and phoneme-grapheme correspondences, concept-word relationships in text, word recognition in isolation, and word recognition in context. Spelling assessments often are administered to obtain information on students' knowledge of spelling features and word patterns. Words are grouped by patterns of increasing difficulty to determine developmental levels in word knowledge.

Fluency in oral reading usually is associated with reading measured for accuracy, automaticity, and prosody. Students are expected to read words in large, meaningful phrase groups and to read with enough ease and without undue attention to decoding so they can focus on text meaning rather than merely word calling. Assessments in fluency measure the use of phonics, vocabulary knowledge, and syntax and the demonstration of comprehension through inflection.

Vocabulary, the ability to understand and use words accurately, is essential in all literacies. McKenna and Stahl (2003) suggest that it may be the best predictor of comprehension. Teachers can use pretests of possible difficult words before reading. They can also measure vocabulary knowledge by assessing students' ability to use word parts to decipher meanings and to take advantage of situational clues to understand a word's meaning in context.

Reading comprehension, or the accurate reconstruction of the intended meaning from a written text, is the basis for all reading instruction. It is the reason why students learn to decode and build vocabulary and struggle with difficult processes. Monitoring students' use of a variety of comprehension strategies will help teachers ensure that students have access to all means to become proficient readers. It is important to evaluate students' abilities not only to answer questions but also to generate their own questions to a text. In addition, they should be able to summarize and find main ideas and themes and to analyze, generalize, and think critically about what they have read.

Assessments in each of these literacy elements that are directly connected to reading instruction are covered in greater detail in Chapter 3, where specific reading assessment models are explored.

Reasons for Listening and Speaking Assessments

The earliest process in literacy learning is the skill of listening for imitation and for constructing meaning. At the very youngest ages, children listen to animal sounds and practice naming the animal with the picture. They also enjoy "reading along" with audiobooks and learn to turn the pages with a sound signal. Importantly, they use their early phonological awareness to build correspondence between letters and sounds. However, we often take for granted the importance of assessing and monitoring listening and speaking skills once students are capable of efficiently decoding a basic litany of words and have become silent readers and social communicators.

There are a variety of uses for oral assessments in all grades. Certainly, phonemic awareness and phonics lessons in primary oral decoding come to mind. Phonemic awareness, the ability to differentiate the sounds (phonemes) that make up spoken words and to focus on and manipulate phonemes in word pronunciation, is essential in learning to read. The notion that early instruction in systematic phonics significantly facilitates reading achievement has been supported by numerous studies (Ehri, Nunes, Stahl, & Willows, 2001). However, through listening assessments teachers can also determine correct understanding of new vocabulary, literal and inferential comprehension, and critical views held by students. Indeed, students' knowledge often is greater than what they are able to demonstrate in a written context.

Listening comprehension usually is the first important link to building background knowledge. Sometimes a student's silent reading comprehension may be quite low because of a lack of sufficient word knowledge or an inability to decode or recognize words. However, the student's skill at understanding the text when receiving the information orally may be higher, in part because of preexisting background knowledge and oral vocabulary. Much research supports the importance of background knowledge of concepts and topics before reading and writing. One of the most efficient ways of assessing and then building on this background is through listening and speaking.

An important reason to continue listening assessments, even in the later grades, is to help students understand the questions or items on all forms of assessment. Bruner (1960) notes that although students may often provide a correct answer, it is sometimes to the wrong question. Although some students can recall information or locate it within a text by rereading and perhaps even draw reasonable inferential and analytical conclusions, unless they can determine what a test item is asking, they are unable to demonstrate this thinking. Content area assessments also include items framed in ways that do not always allow students to demonstrate what they know because they do not understand what they are being asked to do.

Oral assessments provide a scaffold for later print-based assessments. The most fundamental listening skills require simple recall of story details and facts based on spoken text with simple vocabulary and sentence structure. As students progress to more advanced texts with complicated syntax and more complex vocabulary, the comprehension items require more implicit inferences and analysis from spoken passages. As the passages expand in concept load, the levels of questioning also increase. While students are learning to read and recognize new words at one written level, they must also be working on comprehending strategies on perhaps another oral level of instruction. If we wait for students to be able to accurately decode all the words in their listening vocabularies before we move on to higher-level thinking skills, we run the risk of leaving them further behind as they struggle to catch up in comprehension skills and strategies to their more able classmates once they have mastered the code.

Certainly, before we can expect students to think and respond to text in a written format, they need to be able to listen and speak about their responses and discuss what there is about the text or the question that is confusing. Even in the earliest grades, it is important to help beginning listeners connect literacy to their own ideas. Book clubs, fashioned after older students' literature circles and discussion groups, have proved beneficial, even in preschool contexts (Kvasnicka & Starratt, 2005). Teachers and students control topics and turn taking for different patterns of classroom discourse. Models of reciprocal teaching offer evidence of such practices. Here, students and teachers listen and ask each other questions about the information they have just heard.

In addition, students need practice in receiving, attending to, interpreting, and responding appropriately to verbal messages throughout their school and adult careers. Students must be able to listen accurately, follow spoken directions, discern a speaker's organization and transitional uses, and recognize possible bias in a message. Forms of oral and speaking assessments include evidence of student note taking, teacher anecdotal records or observations, audio and video recordings, rubrics, checklists, and evaluation forms.

Reasons for Visual Assessments

Huey (1908/1915) recommended that students should begin writing by using pictures to stand for words until the use of written words could be substituted for all illustrations. Functional text, including signs and letters, was suggested as a means of introducing children to writing. In the 1930s and 1940s comic pages in newspapers and comic books used a combination of text and pictorial representations to provide literary entertainment. In addition, the panels with pictures and text that are characteristic of this format were used to disseminate serious information on the war and other international news. The military even included training information on field sanitation and war machinery through comic-strip format with both visuals and text (Purves, 1998).

Currently, literacy is undergoing a transformation from printed pages to digital displays and multimedia forms of reading, writing, speaking, and listening to communicate and to understand concepts and ideas. Additional literacy skills are needed to produce and understand the graphic and verbal medium of the World Wide Web, with its animation and video presentations of text. Students' ability to evaluate visual materials on Web sites as reliable representations of information is critical to engaging in today's new literacies.

Maps, tables, and graphs are used increasingly to present information not just as a supplement but as a primary focus of the text, and the importance of understanding the relationship between graphics and text has extended to even the youngest learners. Flowcharts, graphic organizers, and diagrams can communicate processes in much more complete and complex ways than words alone. Data represented through charts, matrices, and spreadsheets can become the basis for initial and continued understanding of content material.

Students must be able to locate and interpret pieces of information in a visual representation and also to fill in missing information when necessary. Additional visual skills include summarizing information depicted in a graphic and understanding how two visuals are interrelated and how they may point to trends in information. In addition, as with Web-based information, students must be capable of discerning relevant, reliable information from distracters and also drawing accurate conclusions and making good decisions based on the visual data.

Some assessment items might measure students' ability to retrieve and read data from a graphic. Others might supply a visual representation or a video program from which students are required to interpret data or a process. Student performance assessments sometimes provide directions for drawing and labeling objects such as an insect and its parts or direct students to translate drawings or diagrams into words. Assessment items may direct students to create a diagram or flowchart that defines a process. In later grades, test takers may be required to locate and use information as they interpret a graph, table, or chart, or they might be required to construct a pictorial to define a concept such as motion or design a floor plan or map to provide directions. In addition, they may be asked to compare, summarize, analyze, and synthesize information presented in related graphics.

FINAL THOUGHTS

Analogies

listening : speaking :: reading : _____

or

road map : journey :: assessments : _____

Tests in literacy achievement can and should serve students and teachers well. Like a road map, they should provide direction to the predetermined objectives. They can also verify individual strengths and weaknesses, document student progress, inform teachers about instruction, and provide information to parents and administrators.

Assessments should encourage students to think, listen, discuss, read, and write in ways to clarify understanding and improve learning. They should inform instruction by providing snapshots of progress and areas for further instruction and development and supplying students with opportunities to explain, interpret, analyze, critique, and research important topics. In addition, large-scale assessments offer parents, policymakers, and the general public information about schools to ensure continued instructional progress for all students.

Assessments certainly are more than testing. They are a mode of discourse in learning that provides teachers with guideposts for decision making based on student understanding. It is important to remember that assessments should be designed to accommodate the needs of student learning and teacher instruction, not the reverse. The results of these assessments can be used to plan and adjust instruction and to provide key feedback to students and parents. In a global community that is based on information and communication, measuring students' abilities to navigate and to effectively use the literacies available to them is essential in ensuring their future success.

REFERENCES

Almack, J. C., & Lang, A. R. (1925). *Problems of the teaching profession.* Boston: Houghton Mifflin.

Bruner, J. (1960). *The process of education.* Cambridge, MA: Harvard University Press.

Caldwell, O. W., & Courtis, S. A. (1971). *Then and now in education 1845–1923: A message of encouragement from the past to the present.* New York: Arno Press & The New York Times. (Original work published 1925)

Ehri, L. C., Nunes, S. R., Stahl, S. A., & Willows, D. M. (2001). Systematic phonics instruction helps students learn to read: Evidence from the National Reading Panel's meta-analysis. *Review of Educational Research, 71*(3), 393–447.

Harris, T. L., & Hodges, R. E. (Eds.). (1995). *The literacy dictionary: The vocabulary of reading and writing.* Newark, DE: International Reading Association.

Huey, E. B. (1915). *The psychology and pedagogy of reading with a review of the history of reading and writing and of methods, texts, and hygiene of reading.* New York: Macmillan. (Original work published in 1908)

International Reading Association and National Council of Teachers of English. (1996). *Standards for the English language arts.* Urbana, IL & Newark, DE: Authors. Also available online at http://www.ncte.org/about/over/standards/110846.htm

Johnson, C. (1907). *The country school.* New York: Thomas Y. Crowell.

Kvasnicka, K., & Starratt, J. (2005). *Book club for preschool: Reading, writing, and talking about books is fun!* Manuscript submitted for publication.

McKenna, M. C., & Stahl, S. A. (2003). *Assessment for reading instruction.* New York: Guilford.

National Council for the Social Studies. (1994). *Expectations of excellence: Curriculum standards for social studies.* Washington, DC: Author.

National Council of Teachers of Mathematics. (1991). *Professional standards for teaching mathematics.* Reston, VA: Author.

National Research Council. (1996). *National science education standards: Observe, interact, change, learn.* Washington, DC: National Academy Press.

Purves, A. (1998). Flies in the web of hypertext. In D. Reinking, M. C. McKenna, L. D. Labbo, & R. D. Kieffer (Eds.), *Handbook of literacy and technology: Transformations in a post-typographic world* (pp. 235–251). Mahwah, NJ: Erlbaum.

Smith, N. B. (1970). *American reading instruction: Its development and its significance in gaining a perspective on current practices in reading.* Newark, DE: International Reading Association. (Original work published in 1934)

Taylor, J. M. (2005). *A history of written composition instruction in U.S. elementary schools to 1945.* Unpublished doctoral dissertation, University of Nevada, Reno.

Venezky, R. L. (1984). The history of reading research. In P. D. Pearson, R. Barr, M. L. Kamil, & P. Mosenthal (Eds.), *Handbook of reading research* (pp. 3–38). New York: Longman.

2

Writing Assessments

How much writing instruction occurred when you were a student in school? When your parents were in the same grades? How about your grandparents? Did they receive the same kind of writing lessons you are teaching or you learned as a student?

Recently, national and state testing systems have focused on writing instruction not only by assessing students' ability to write extended text to a provided prompt but also by including open-ended response items to the already familiar multiple-choice items in their content test format. That testing practice, along with the electronic communication industry using writing as a common means of requesting and exchanging information, has increased the importance of writing instruction in curriculum planning and assessments.

BRIEF HISTORICAL OVERVIEW OF WRITING ASSESSMENTS

In the early twentieth century, Edward L. Thorndike, one of the most noted psychologists of that century, and Milo B. Hillegas, his associate, assembled a series of composition examples from which student samples could be measured, compared, and scaled (Thorndike, 1911). Using the graded writing samples of papers judged on the basis of form and content by "a considerable number of competent judges" (Noyes, 1912, p. 533), evaluators would need only to match a student sample with the graded examples to determine a uniform grade. Later, these scales, better known as the Hillegas scales, were revised and expanded to begin the evolving science of writing assessment that has continued to the present.

As early as 1916, holistic scoring scales based first on form and content and then on mechanics were included in some fifth- and sixth-grade textbooks, along with rubrics and annotated models defining the scores (Hosic & Hooper, 1916, 1932). Students were encouraged to collect this scored work in portfolios to demonstrate progress and to reread at the end of the year (Figure 2.1). Short-answer assessments and limited writing assessments as directed by workbook

Figure 2.1   Portfolio Instructions for Fourth Through Sixth Grades, 1916

A PORTFOLIO FOR MANUSCRIPTS

II. You will find it desirable to have a portfolio in which to keep your manuscripts. Study the cut that appears on this page, and follow the instructions given.

If you use smaller composition paper than foolscap, you should have a smaller portfolio than the one provided for. Make your own measurements.

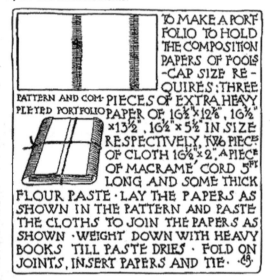

NOTE: From *A Child's Composition Book* (p. 11), by J. F. Hosic and C. R. Hooper, 1916, Chicago: Rand McNally.

formats were also in evidence during this time (McFadden, 1912). These student exercise books, dealing with both convergent and divergent writing tasks, became a popular means of assessing reading and writing for the rest of the century.

During the postwar baby boom of the 1950s, standardized, norm-referenced tests, rather than the previously used essay exams, became well established as a means of assessing student writing proficiency through indirect measures; that is, students were asked to choose correct responses from multiple choices to determine best composition practices. Undoubtedly this was due in part to the ease of administering and scoring the work of large numbers of students.

Around the mid-1960s, assessment in literacy began to change as criterion-referenced measurements attempted to demonstrate better alignment with behavioral outcome models than the previously and exclusively used norm-referenced tests (Johnston, 1984), and the use of direct writing assessments became popular. Students were again being asked to respond in writing to an assigned topic or prompt, and papers were scored by teachers who had received special training in scoring accurately and consistently.

WRITING ASSESSMENTS TODAY

As she collects materials from the supply room, Bianca, a middle school English teacher, discusses the successes she is having with her students in some writing assignments. Fred, a social studies teacher, is contemplating an integrated unit that he and Bianca are planning to teach together during the next semester.

"You know," says Bianca as she flips through the student papers, looking at the comments she has attached with stick-on notes, "I think they really understand the concept of style. They also seem to have a sense of audience and purpose. This class is much better than last year's class. They're really a great deal smarter."

"Do you think so?" asks Fred. "Although I like this group much better and they're certainly more attentive than last year's wild bunch, I'm not so sure they're smarter or even farther along in content material. Have you checked their folders for test results yet? Rick was sharing some of their math scores with me yesterday, and although some of the individual students are exceptionally higher or lower than last year's group, they are pretty much at the same level overall. I'm going to take a closer look at all their reading and writing scores later this week. Do you want to join me?"

Without an adequate means of describing student achievement and comparing it between cohorts of students, educators may make subjective judgments about student achievement and the best methods of determining instruction. A variety of standardized writing assessment measures and models can assist in evaluating student proficiencies in writing tasks.

The National Assessment of Educational Progress (NAEP) program began assessing student writing according to the direct method during the 1969-1970 school year. Their methods and research have provided models for state and district assessment practices that have evolved to present-day testing procedures. Today, the program provides information on 4th-, 8th-, and 12th-grade student writing with direct writing assessments using a national random sample population. The NAEP report describes student achievement levels as *basic, proficient,* or *advanced* on narrative, informational, and persuasive writing tasks based on expected performance standards. See Table 2.1 for NAEP achievement levels. The next national writing assessment for grades 8 and 12 will be held in 2007, and the next national writing assessment for grades 4 and 8 will be held in 2011. For more information on NAEP assessments, visit their Web site (http://nces.ed.gov/nationsreportcard/about/).

Standardized trait writing assessment models, popularized by educators Vicki Spandel and Ruth Culham, are available at the Northwest Regional Educational Laboratory Web site (http://www.nwrel.org). Today's state assessments often are modeled after national rubric models that provide guidelines for reliable instruments for determining student levels of proficiency and progress.

TYPES OF WRITING ASSESSMENTS

Two types of writing assessment formats are popular today: objective and direct. Objective writing assessments use selected-response (multiple-choice) formats to measure discrete aspects of writing, usually involving usage, mechanics, sentence structure, and vocabulary, and revision possibilities for sentence organization within a paragraph. See Table 2.2 for examples of objective writing assessment items.

(Text continues on page 24)

Table 2.1 NAEP Achievement Level Descriptions by Traits and Grade Levels

	4th Grade			8th Grade			12th Grade		
	Basic	Proficient	Advanced	Basic	Proficient	Advanced	Basic	Proficient	Advanced
General: Audience and purpose	Demonstrates somewhat organized and detailed response based on allowable time limits; shows a general grasp of the assigned writing task.	Demonstrates organized response that shows understanding of the writing task; shows awareness of expected audience through form, content, and language.	Demonstrates effective, well-developed response based on allowable time limits; shows clear understanding of the writing task and the expected audience.	Demonstrates effective response based on allowable time limits; shows a general understanding of the assigned writing task and awareness of expected audience.	Demonstrates a detailed and organized response based on allowable time limits; shows clear understanding of the writing task and the expected audience.	Demonstrates fully developed response based on allowable time limits; shows clear understanding of the writing task and expected audience.	Demonstrates well-organized response based on allowable time limits; shows an understanding of both the assigned writing task and the expected audience.	Demonstrates effectively organized and fully developed response based on allowable time limits; shows clear understanding of writing task and expected audience.	Demonstrates mature, sophisticated response based on allowable time limits; evidence of ability to engage audience.
Details	Includes some supporting details.	Includes details that support and develop the main idea.	Includes details and elaboration that support main idea.	Includes supporting details in an organized way.	Makes use of details and some elaboration to support and develop main idea.	Includes details and elaboration to support and develop main idea.	Includes supporting details for the main idea.	Includes details and elaboration to support and develop main idea.	Includes details and elaboration to support fully developed main idea.
Organization	Is somewhat organized.	Is organized.	Is clearly organized, using consistency of topic or theme, sequencing or clearly marked beginning and ending.	Includes supporting details in an organized way.	Is organized, making use of sequencing or clearly marked beginning and ending.	Clearly and consistently organized effect.	Is clearly organized, making use of techniques such as consistency in topic or theme, sequencing, and a clear	Is organized and coherent, using techniques such as consistent theme, sequencing, and clear	Is well crafted, with coherent effect.

	4th Grade			8th Grade			12th Grade		
	Basic	Proficient	Advanced	Basic	Proficient	Advanced	Basic	Proficient	Advanced
							introduction and conclusion.	introduction and conclusion.	
Language and sentence structure		Is appropriate to audience.	Uses precise and varied language.		Uses precise language and some variety of sentence structure.	Demonstrates precise word choice and varied sentence structure.	Shows some analytical, evaluative, or creative thinking.	Uses precise language and variety of sentence structure.	Uses rich and compelling language, precise word choice, and variety in sentence structure.
Thinking skills			May show analytical, evaluative, or creative thinking.		May show analytical, evaluative, or creative thinking.	Shows some analytical, evaluative, or creative thinking.		Shows analytical, evaluative, or creative thinking.	Uses analytical, evaluative, or creative thinking.
Literary strategies						May use literary strategies (e.g., analogies, illustrations, examples, anecdotes, figurative language) to clarify a point.			Uses literary strategies (e.g., anecdotes, repetition) to develop ideas.

(Continued)

Table 2.1 (Continued)

	4th Grade			8th Grade			12th Grade		
	Basic	*Proficient*	*Advanced*	*Basic*	*Proficient*	*Advanced*	*Basic*	*Proficient*	*Advanced*
Conventions	Grammar, spelling, and capitalization are accurate enough to communicate to a reader, although there may be mistakes that get in the way of meaning.	Grammar, spelling, and capitalization are accurate enough to communicate to a reader; although some mistakes are present, they do not distort meaning.	Grammar, spelling, capitalization are accurate enough to communicate clearly; mistakes are so few and minor that they are easily skimmed over.	Grammar, spelling, punctuation, and capitalization are accurate enough to communicate to a reader, although there may be mistakes that get in the way of meaning.	Grammar, spelling, punctuation, and capitalization are accurate enough to communicate to a reader; although some mistakes are present, they do not distort meaning.	Grammar, spelling, punctuation, capitalization, and sentence structure contain few errors; control of conventions may be used for stylistic effect.	Grammar, spelling, and capitalization are accurate enough to communicate to a reader; although some mistakes are present, they do not distort meaning.	Grammar, spelling, punctuation, capitalization, and sentence structure contain few errors; command of conventions may be used for stylistic effect.	Grammar, spelling, punctuation, capitalization, and sentence structure contain few errors; sophisticated command of conventions may be used for stylistic effect.

NOTE: Adapted from NAEP 1998 Report Card for the Nation of the States.

Table 2.2   Examples of Objective Writing Assessment Tasks

---

(1) Over the past two decades, pigs have increased in their popularity as household pets in the United States. **(2)** Since pigs are affectionate animals. **(3)** They love companionship and body contact. **(4)** Like most domesticated pets they need a balanced diet they need clean water they need the right type of living environment. **(5)** They also need a health program that includes regular medical check-ups and vaccinations. **(6)** If a pet pig is allowed to exercise regularly, is not overfed, and is examined and cared for annually by a veterinarian, he/she should live to a ripe old age of 15 to 30 years.

1. **How is sentence (4) *best* written?**
    a. Like most domesticated pets, they need a balanced diet, clean water, and the right type of living environment.
    b. Like most domesticated pets they need a balanced diet they need clean water they need the right type of living environment.
    c. Like most domesticated pets they need a balanced diet and they need clean water and they need the right type of living environment.
    d. Like most domesticated pets they need a balanced diet and they need clean water. And they need the right type of living environment.

2. **Which of the sentences is *not* a complete sentence?**
    a. Sentence (1)
    b. Sentence (2)
    c. Sentence (3)
    d. Sentence (4)

Sample Passage

(7) One problem with pigs is they will eat just about anything. **(8)** That's where the expression, "eats like a pig," comes from! **(9)** Unlike cats, which they will usually stop eating when they are full, pigs can eat themselves sick. **(10)** They may also, if given the chance, eat things that can be harmful to them or even fatal. **(11)** <u>Besides</u>, pet owners should be careful to "pig-proof" their pet's living area to make sure their pig only eats a healthful diet.

3. **Choosing from the words below, pick a better linking word than *Besides* for sentence (11).**
    a. Instead
    b. However
    c. Therefore
    d. For example

4. **How is sentence (9) best written?**
    a. Unlike cats, which will usually stop eating when they are full, pigs can eat itself sick.
    b. Unlike cats, which will usually stop eating when it is full, pigs can eat themselves sick.
    c. Unlike cats, which will usually stop eating when they are full, pigs can eat themselves sick.
    d. Unlike a cat, which will usually stop eating when they are full, pigs can eat themselves sick.

Sample Passage

(12) Pigs can be taught to perform tricks with food as a reward. **(13)** Dogs are more playful than pigs. **(14)** Frozen grapes and cucumber slices make good treats for tricks well done or lessons well learned. **(15)** Other good treats are air-popped popcorn (plain, no butter), carrot slices, and individual pieces of dry cereal like Cheerios and Chex.

(Continued)

Table 2.2 (Continued)

---

(16) Owning a pet pig is somewhat like being a parent. (17) Patience and love are required; and owners must remain patient with their small charges. (18) However, the rewards for companionship and friendship are great with this communicative, affectionate, and intelligent animal.

5. **In which of the following sentences is the same thing said twice?**

   a. Sentence 15: Other good treats are air-popped popcorn (plain, no butter), carrot slices, and individual pieces of dry cereal like Cheerios and Chex.
   b. Sentence 16: Owning a pet pig is somewhat like being a parent.
   c. Sentence 17: Patience and love are required; and owners must not become annoyed with their small charges.
   d. Sentence 18: However, the rewards for companionship and friendship are great with this communicative, affectionate, and intelligent animal.

6. **Which sentence does not belong in the passage?**

   a. Sentence 12
   b. Sentence 13
   c. Sentence 14
   d. Sentence 15

Many computer word processing programs can be used to objectively assess spelling and grammar and provide counts of errors, words, characters, sentences, and paragraphs. They can also give information on average characters per word, words per sentence, and sentences per paragraph that are sometimes part of readability data studies. These assessments sometimes are compared with large populations to rank student performance, or they can be part of a criterion-referenced testing system that has defined standards on which students must demonstrate proficiency. This indirect type of writing assessment is criticized for its emphasis on the identification rather than the effective use of essential writing elements.

The direct method of writing assessment is based on actual production of student writing. Students are provided with a writing task through a set of instructions and are expected to generate writing that will be evaluated on specified criteria. These assignments sometimes are timed. As seen in Figure 2.2, the range of composing restraints associated with this type of writing can vary from student-selected divergent to teacher-directed convergent writing. The tasks themselves can range from untimed divergent responses, with much student choice in idea development and with revisions based on feedback, to a narrower, convergent response in which single-focused responses are expected based on individual, timed responses. This last type is especially prevalent where writing is used to assess other content areas. Individual student papers may be evaluated, or sets of papers may be included in portfolios of student work as explained more fully in Chapter 5.

In terms of validity, both types of assessments, direct and indirect, can be deemed valid as long as they reflect what is being taught. According to testing expert Edward M. White (1994), the key to validity is that the assessments allow all writers to demonstrate their best efforts.

Figure 2.2   Continuum of Writing Tasks

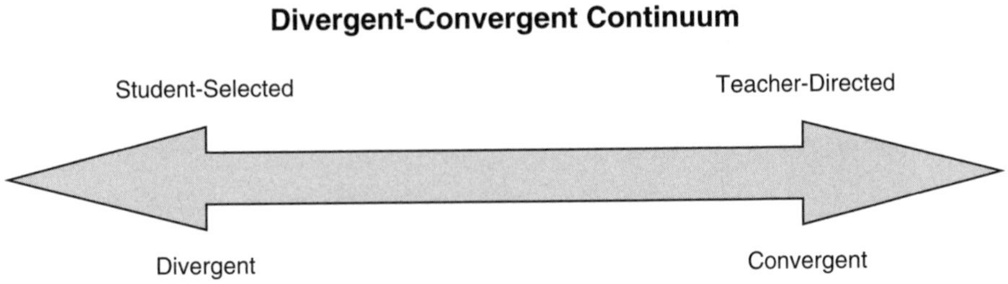

Divergent-Convergent Continuum

Student-Selected   Teacher-Directed

Divergent   Convergent

Types of assessments also vary depending on the audiences and purposes of the writing assessments. High-stakes state and district assessments often are used for summative evaluation purposes, and their audiences usually are policymakers, educational administrators, and the general public. These assessments generally are used for accountability to determine student achievement and teacher or program effectiveness. On the other hand, low-stakes formative assessments usually are based on instructional needs. Students can self-assess based on rubrics and models, peers can provide feedback based on peer-evaluation activities, and teachers can confer with students to provide instructional guidance in perfecting writing performance. Formative assessments tend to pay more attention to process, whereas summative assessments are concerned solely with the product of writing efforts.

WRITING TASKS

Writing Forms

Forms of writing used in writing assessments often are based on the purpose defined by the writing prompt. For example, narrative writing often is used in students' fictional and nonfictional story or essay writing based on prompts or in response to provided texts or visuals. Expository writing, in which students create informative text, can also be based on provided texts or visuals, in this case informational items such as charts or diagrams, newspaper articles, or informational texts. Functional, how-to types of writing are also classified as informational writing. Functional texts such as diagrams and charts, tables, graphs, and pictures are examples of the types of text students must learn to understand and produce on their own. Persuasive writing, in which students generate and support reasons for action or changes in attitude, sometimes are written in letter-writing formats but usually are presented in essay style. Diagrams and charts can be used to help clarify a sequence or illustrate a point.

Assessment Prompt Formats

"What a stupid assignment this is," complained Juan. "I can't believe we have to write about what we did on our summer vacation again! We write about it every year, and every year I have the same stupid nothing to write about."

"I know," responded Dimi. "When I was little, I could talk about the fun time I had in the park or how I played with my friends, but now that we're older, what are we supposed to say? That we had amazing adventures cleaning the house with our mothers, or we watched TV and played video games until we were sick of them?"

"Hey, maybe we should make something up. You know, like we slipped out our bedroom windows every night to fight crime. Or how about if I talk about how I joined a drug ring and led the gang out of danger from a police raid? Now that would a good one, huh?"

One of us, in our youth, actually did respond to this prompt in a manner similar to Juan's in this example and received an early lesson on the importance of knowing your audience when the good Sisters of St. Joseph failed to find the story amusing.

Is there a more reliable (or boring) writing prompt than *What I Did on My Summer Vacation*? Generations of student writers have had to contend with this time-honored topic. Like most clichés, in primary grades it may indeed seem novel and provide a real reason for writing with authenticity. However, by the time students are in the intermediate grades, they often respond with groans of annoyance, and their low levels of enthusiasm often are reflected in their written responses.

The search for readily available and reliable writing prompt models has been an issue at least since the early nineteenth century. Textbooks from that time reveal attempts to provide teachers and students with many possible writing topics. For example, Richard Green Parker (1833) provided more than 300 possible topics on which students could write, perhaps contributing to the successful publication and reprinting of his composition textbooks well into the late nineteenth century. Topics range from simple one-word prompts, usually abstract nouns such as *Adversity, Wit, Ocean,* or *Art,* to short, often pithy sayings on which to elaborate, such as *Trust Not Appearances* or *Never Too Old to Learn,* in addition to descriptions of geographic destinations and histories of concrete objects such as *History of a Needle.*

Teachers and test administrators continue to struggle with the difficulties in designing testing prompts that all students can understand easily and to which they can respond quickly in written formats. Wolcott and Legg (1998) warn that topics must be written to evoke interest but not produce such an emotional response that writers lose control of their writing. White (1994) notes the difficulties in providing a level field for students from different cultures and with varied background knowledge when choosing topics for large-scale assessments.

Today's writing prompts usually consist of an introduction or opening remark followed by directions for writing. The instructions might include a literary work, quotation, photograph, drawing, cartoon, diagram, chart, or task. They can measure students' proficiency in the craft of writing and can also be used within content areas to allow students to demonstrate knowledge of content materials or processes.

Divergent Writing Prompts

Divergent prompts are used most often in writing tasks designed to measure students' competence in writing skills. They vary from personal-experience narratives, thought by some to be the easiest, to analytical expository or persuasive texts, often seen as the most difficult (White, 1994). These prompts offer a variety of choices within specific guidelines and criteria. They vary from the very open assignments that simply instruct students to write in any form on a self-selected topic to more explicit but still flexible topics, such as, "Many people have a special place they like to visit. Describe a special place you like to visit and explain why it is special to you." Item writers expect that every student will have something to say about such a topic but that not all responses will be the same.

Practicing with a selection of predetermined prompts based on previous assessments can limit students in their ability to deal with divergent topics while they are taking tests and when they are required to determine their own topics (Graves, 1983). Instead, teachers need to guide students in making a divergent writing prompt their own by analyzing the topic in terms of their own background and experiences.

Students need practice in self-selecting topics that interest them personally so they can think and write about meaningful things that are connected to the prompts. For example, many students in our schools write about soccer. It is their favorite sport, and they have stories and information to write about it. When they are prompted to write about a favorite place, they choose the soccer field, and they have vocabulary and ideas to match the prompt. If they are directed to write about something they do well, they can also write about a single event in which they excelled in soccer. Helping students understand how a divergent prompt is designed to support them in telling about what they already know shows them how to focus on crafting a piece of writing with authentic ideas, organization, and style suited to their needs.

We help our students practice revision by using their previous writings to write to the new prompt. This allows them to see that they can have something familiar to say about a provided topic and also gives them practice with timed tests and editing skills associated with the tests. See Table 2.3 for a list of divergent writing prompts we have used with students in helping them revisit their writing and make prompts their own.

Convergent Writing Prompts

Convergent prompts, being more concisely focused, are more likely to be used in assessing student achievement in content areas such as reading, math, science, the social sciences, and the arts. They are closely aligned to content-standard indicators and provide the means by which attainment of specific standards is measured. Expected student responses usually are quite uniform and may range from dictation to items that call for student-based logic and reasoning, as framed in a content area. For example, in reading, students may be asked to retell or summarize a piece of text, or they may be required to explain the main idea or theme of the story. In addition, they might be required to make inferences or take a critical stance, based on information in the passage.

Convergent prompts may be structured to allow multipart answers. For example, "There are two main characters in the story. (A) Explain the ways in which they are the same. (B) Explain the ways in which they are different."

Table 2.3   Divergent Writing Prompts

Narrative

1. We are learning new things all the time. Write about a time when you learned something new.

2. Write about an experience in which you were proud of the way you thought and acted.

3. Each school day we stop for lunch. Write about an experience you have had during lunchtime at school.

4. Imagine coming to school one morning to find that a large and beautiful castle has appeared on the school playground. Write a story about what happens at school that day.

5. One day you arrive in your classroom to find a large box on the teacher's desk. Sounds are coming from the box, and it is shaking slightly. Tell what happens next.

6. Friends can play an important part in our lives. Tell about a time when you made a new friend.

7. Life is filled with large and small adventures. Write about a large or small adventure you have had.

8. Sometimes things happen, fortunately, just at the right time. Tell about a time when something happened to you or to someone else at just the right time. Provide enough details for readers to understand what it was like.

9. Sometimes things that have become lost are found again. Tell about a time when you or someone you know lost something and then found it. Describe the lost item and the experience as completely as you can.

10. Some things in life happen that are unplanned surprises. Write about a time when you were surprised. Write about this experience so that your reader can understand it clearly.

Expository

1. There are many important things in our world. Explain something you know about that is important.

2. Each day you come to school hoping for the best day possible. Explain all the things that could happen during a day at school that would make it a perfect day.

3. Think about an activity that you enjoy doing. Explain it so someone else could understand why you enjoy it.

4. There are interesting places all around us. Tell about a place that is interesting to you. It could be a place you have been to or heard about, or it could be an imaginary place. Be sure to include specific details showing what makes the place interesting.

5. Think about a favorite time for you. It could be a season of the year or a special day. Explain why that time is important to you.

6. You have learned many important things in school this year. Write a letter to a student who will be in your grade next year and explain one important thing that they will learn next year and why it is important.

7. One day you come to school and have a substitute teacher. Write him or her a letter explaining some important things to know about your class and school day and why these things are important to know.

8. Think of something you have done or have seen someone else do that was difficult but worthwhile. Tell about it. Explain it so clearly that your audience will understand what you know about it.

9. There are many exciting things to see in our world. Explain something you have seen or learned about that was exciting. Include details so your readers will feel as if they are seeing or learning about the same thing.

10. Both in school and out of school, we have many opportunities to attend interesting events. Explain about an interesting event you have attended and what made it so interesting.

Persuasive

1. Many books are fun to read. Write about some reasons why other people should read your favorite book.

2. There are many heroes who are recognized in our world today. Think about what being a hero means, and explain who your personal hero is and why.

3. Objects sometimes are used to represent groups of people. Select an object that might be used to represent American life today and explain why it is a good choice.

4. Some people think that too much emphasis is placed on sports in schools today. Explain why you think this is true or false and persuade your readers to agree with you.

5. Think about some improvement for your school. It might be a new class or some item that will improve your school site. Giving specific reasons, write and convince your principal that your improvement idea is a good one.

6. Your teacher has decided to get a class pet. Think about what would be the perfect pet for your classroom. Write a letter to your teacher persuading him or her to get the pet of your choice. Make sure to give good reasons that will convince your teacher.

7. All four seasons have good reasons for being our favorites. Pick *one* season and tell why it is your favorite. Include examples so your readers will agree with your choice.

8. Field trips can be fun and educational. Think of a good field trip for your class. Write to your teacher and convince her or him to take your class on this field trip. Remember to include good reasons so your teacher will be persuaded.

9. Some people prefer to live in small cities or in rural areas. Other people prefer to live in large cities. Tell about the one place where you would like to live. Provide reasons to persuade your readers that your choice is best.

10. You and a friend have some free time to spend together. You would like to do one activity (pick a real one) and he or she would like to do another (pick a different real one). Persuade your friend to choose your activity instead of the other one.

In math, convergent prompts might ask students to solve a problem, show their work, and explain their answers, or they might be required to write a rule for a given pattern or explain how to best estimate a solution. They might also be asked to use words to compare and contrast data or geometric figures.

In science, they may be asked to apply scientific knowledge by constructing diagrams, graphs, or pictorials and explaining the principles or concepts being illustrated, or they might be asked to compare, contrast, or analyze scientific concepts. As in math, students often are required to explain their conceptual understanding as well as to show basic knowledge of facts.

Both divergent and convergent tasks are designed to provide a window into student knowledge and reasoning. The process of developing appropriate and useful writing prompts takes practice and attention to the entire learning process. See Table 2.4 for a checklist to help you in writing convergent and divergent writing prompts.

In addition, after multiple experiences with writing prompts, students and teachers should assess the prompts themselves. Did they achieve their purpose? Which seem to be the easiest for individual students? Why might that be? Collaborative teacher-student input into topic development helps students define their own strengths and weaknesses with various topics and formats, helps them determine how to deal with difficult topics, and prepares them for test anxiety on writing assessments. It also validates the reliability of the items for subsequent use.

EVALUATION TOOLS

Exemplars

Mrs. Cameron's third-grade class tromps into the room from recess. Heavy boots, jackets, and scarves have been discarded in the hallway. The chilly January weather and jump-rope activity have left them breathless as they enter the room. Mrs. Cameron joined them at recess today to turn the rope and chant some of the jump rope rhymes they wrote in class earlier.

After much laughter and sharing of the recess experience, Mrs. Cameron asks, "Marisol, how did you learn to jump rope so well?"

Marisol replies shyly. "I don't know. I guess I just watched other girls jumping, mostly my big sister's friends, and then I tried it myself."

Mrs. Cameron asks, "How many of you have ever practiced a trick you saw someone else do first?"

Many hands shoot up from both boys and girls.

"Well," she continues, "that is what we are going to do today with writing. We are going to pay attention to what the writer of this story did well. Then we are going to practice some of those things with our own writing."

The use of excellent writing models, taken from age-appropriate literature, is one of the most time-honored practices of writing instruction. As students evaluate the qualities of a good piece of writing and practice these techniques in their own ways, they are apprenticing themselves, much as artists work with masters. Student insights into the power of word pictures and how they engage

Table 2.4   Checklist for Developing Divergent and Convergent Writing Prompts

Divergent

Is the topic sufficiently interesting and appropriate for all members in this group of students?

Are the audience and purpose clearly defined?

In writing to this topic myself, what difficulties did I encounter? What problems do I believe my students may have with writing to this topic?

Are students familiar with examples of proficient writing similar to this?

Will this assignment be used to measure process? Product? Both process and product?

How much support will students receive from instructors or peers at any stage of this writing? Prewriting? Drafting? Revision? Copyediting?

Will response to this writing assignment occur all at once or be spread out over several periods of time?

Has there been adequate explanation and practice in understanding the expectations for successful completion of this writing?

Is a rubric or checklist attached to the assignment?

Convergent

What do I want my students to know and be able to do based on the curriculum and tied to the standards?

What content and assessments have occurred before this assessment?

What content and assessments will be occurring after this assessment?

Have we devoted sufficient time and effort to this content, using literacy to define, explain, and elaborate, so that students can demonstrate their proficiency?

Can this content best be assessed through the use of an open-ended, written format?

What are my expectations for student writing for this item?

Does the item provide adequate information for students to understand clearly the expectations for correct responses?

Is the item structured in such a way that it is manageable to answer?

What does my own written response to the item indicate are important components of a minimally correct response? Of an exemplary response?

them as readers are the reader-writer connection that distinguishes merely proficient writing from excellent writing. Students can underline golden lines or phrases and, after discussing and analyzing how these techniques may work, can incorporate some of them into revisions of their own work.

The Hillegas scales, mentioned earlier in this chapter, allowed a range of quality in models for student analysis and emulation. Though not efficient when used solely as scoring guides, student samples are essential accompaniments to scoring rubrics for instructional purposes. In fact, they are the basis for most scoring rubric designs. According to Myers (1980, p. 2), asking teachers "to select typical samples which they rate highly" is the best way to identity good writing. These exemplars can then be used to construct holistic scales and scoring rubrics to assess student writing. A developmental sample of primary student papers is provided in Figure 2.3, and sample anchor papers are used to define high-, medium-, and low-quality papers for Grades 5 and 8 in Table 2.5.

Figure 2.3   Developmental Primary Student Writing Samples

Undefined squiggles and random marks.	Defined scribbling with left-to-right or top-to-bottom progression.	Drawings and pretend letters that may be explained as "That's me and my name right there."
Random letter strings or groups of letters that may resemble words.	*flower* Labeled drawings. Pictures and words that indicate letter–sound matching.	*Exit* Duplication of environmental print; may include reversals.
My dog running Evidence of letter–sound correspondence with initial consonant sounds.	*bird sun* Evidence of beginning and ending sounds.	*I let my dog out.* Evidence of beginning, middle, and ending sounds with vowels by letter name.

The next progression involves writing phrases, then whole sentences, lists, and stories with gradually greater sophistication and complexity.

Table 2.5   Examples of Student Writing

The following papers were written in response to the following prompt given by Aaron Grossman to his fifth-grade class: "You have had many interesting experiences in your life. Tell about an interesting experience you have had. Describe it so your readers can understand it completely."

Fifth Grade: High

I experienced the coolest most amazing feeling on a rollercoaster called Medusa. Let me tell you all about it. I was walking up the stairs of the rollercoaster entrance on the Medusa. I was getting ready to turn around and go running to my mom because when you're going to get on the craziest ride, your stomach feels like it's going to explode! Also it was my "VERY FIRST TIME!" When I was getting ready for running back to my mom two cousins got a hold of me and said, "Don't worry. It'll be fun and just in case if you think you're going to pass out, scream as loud as you can, and in case try not to wet your pants!"

Just when I got in the big long cart, I said to myself, "I hate roller coasters. Why did they have to invent Six Flaaaaaa. . . ." In just that minute the cart ZOOMED so fast my hair tie flew off my hair!

Then slowly the long cart went up a big rollercoaster hill, then zoomed back down on the other side of the hill. It felt like there was a big ball in my stomach with butterflies in it! The ride had loopdaloops and even double loops, even big huge hills and also twisters. When the ride was over it felt like I'd been flying the whole time and when I walked I felt weak. My legs were like jelly. My cousins went on it again, but me, I went running to my mom who asked, "Do you want to go on the ride once more?" "No thanks," I said with a weak smile. "Maybe later."

The writer does an effective job of describing the experience that seems real and convincing. The details are relevant and interesting and provide a unique perspective on the roller coaster ride. Fluent, chronological ordering takes the readers through the writing in a chronological manner, and transitions such as "Just when," "Then slowly," and "When the ride was over" move the reader through the series of events. The writer's style is evident in descriptions and reactions to events in an attempt to engage the audience, and there is evidence of experimenting with words to describe the types of loops and twists of the ride. A variety of sentence structures are present, and although there are some conventional errors in this piece that require copyediting, there is also evidence of mastery of some difficult conventions, such as quotation marks. Overall, this is a well-done piece of writing that showcases an exciting event for this 10-year-old.

Fifth Grade: Medium

Have you ever babysat before? Well if you haven't then I'll tell you my story of babysitting a child named Sally Ann. Well when I told Sally Ann, "Let's play a bored game" she said ok and threw the game in my face. Then for dinner she stuffed the food in my mouth. For TV time she got to watch Dora the explorerdora. Yes, she's 8 years old but still likes to watch it. Dora is about a girl with a monkey who finds different items. Finally it was bed time. She told me to tell her the story of Jack and the Beanstalk. But instead of her falling asleep I fell asleep.

That's my story. But I must warn you babysitting just might be the last event you ever do.

Readers are provided with some specific reasons why it was difficult to babysit Sally Ann, but they seem more like a list and could benefit from some elaboration. Although the introduction is designed to hook the reader, the conclusion doesn't seem to match. If the purpose was to convince readers that they may not ever want to babysit, it is not evident from the introduction. However, there is a clear understanding of the task and satisfactory support for the main idea of the difficulties in babysitting. An individualistic style is evident in some sentences, such as, "Yes, she's 8 years old but" and "That's my story. But I must warn you." Sentence structures are varied, and transitions are used well to move through the events. Conventions are accurate enough to show average control of standard forms and spelling.

(Continued)

Table 2.5 (Continued)

Fifth Grade: Low

One day we wont to a forest with my friends and then we saw a creek. We went in that creek. We swim and my friends know how to swim but I don't know how to swim so then my friends teach me how to swim in the water and then we went to 1 store because we are tired so the stores owner gaves us a bikes. my friends know how to ride a bike but I don't know how to ride a bike. Oh, I forgot to tell my friends names is Alvaro, Anthony, Ariel and me and the we see a school and then we went there and we saw kids and then we went back to our house. When we going to the our home we saw many animals like Elephant, tiger, Deer, Fox, cow and we saw many, many birds like parrots. Oh when I went in the creek we saw baby crocodile and I thing may be when I become big I will be a forest man like the when we watch a T.V like snake master. We went back to our home.

It seems like this piece may be part fantasy and part real, and readers are not provided with enough information to understand the point of the story. Readers aren't sure whether this is a story about a visit to a forest with exotic animals, an explanation about swimming or bicycling lessons, or a visit to school. This writer needs much assistance in focusing on a topic. In part because the topic is so unclear, organization is scattered and difficult to follow. Spelling and punctuation errors are distracting. There is a problem with run-on sentences.

*****

The following papers were written in response to a Nevada State Proficiency Examination prompt for eighth graders: "Describe your favorite childhood toy, object, or place. Describe your choice and tell about it so your reader can understand why it was so important to you."

Eighth Grade: High

In the distant fog of my memories, I remember my childhood. Suddenly, in my mind, I am five years old again. Sitting in the middle of my room, I admire my favorite toy. It looked back at me with its circus clown face, smiling constantly. It was only a doll clown, with a red mouth, button eyes, a ruffle around the neck, and a tall hat.

I pull the string and like magic a bellowing electronic laugh booms out, shattering the silence. It has always kept me company during bad times. During the raging thunderstorms, or the threat of a monster inhabiting my closet, or times when I'm just feeling sad or lonely, I crawl under my bed with my clown and pull the string over and over. And in a short matter of time, the laughing doll will have chased my fears away.

I reflect, and my solemn face cracks a wide smile. To this day, it sits in my quarters, still grinning. I look at the doll, and I grin back. Because I will never, under any circumstances, forget what this childhood toy has done for me.

This expressive piece provides a vivid childhood memory in an individualistic manner, with an effort at creativity and insight. The precise description of the toy along with specific times when it brought comfort places this paper in a high category. The organization moves the reader from the present to the past and back to the present in a clear manner that enhances the central idea. The unconventional syntax seems to be deliberate as a means of control for stylistic effect. Although there is a shift in verb tense between *admire* and *looked*, it is a fairly minor error, and the text is very readable.

Eighth Grade: Medium

As a young child we all had a favorite toy, object or place. As for me I had a soft blue, satin-lined blanky, I loved it so much because I had slept with it every night since I was born, and it kept me warm. It make me feel comfortable and secure to be with it at all times. For about three years I stayed with the blanket. I always loved my blanky because it was really the only thing I desired and could physically manage. When my mom needed to change my diaper I would not let go of my pride and joy.

For some strange reason my blue blanky was washed about one time and was getting dirty, worn and tattered. One day my mom just did away with it, but I never really noticed that it was gone, because the had bought me a new one in replace of it. I will always remember my first joy, my blue, satin-lined blanky.

This paper is adequate in its treatment of the subject. It provides support for the reasons why the blanket is important. However, much of the support is general, and some details seem contrived, such as sleeping with it every night since birth and the diaper change, which sound like anecdotes related to the writer rather than firsthand memories. There are some usage problems, such as pronoun agreement in the first sentence, and misunderstandings about comma usage. Although some spelling errors are present, they do not substantially interfere with meaning, but this paper could benefit from some minor editing.

Eighth Grade: Low
When I was about six years old my faverate toy was my monster truck. I had them scattered all over the house. It it al started when I got one for chrismas from my mother and I liked it a lot. I also got some action figures and bord games. I took care of all my stuff until my little brother came along then he recked things. What a pain!

Information is very limited in this paper and does not focus on a single object. In the first sentence the reader is led to believe the story will be about a monster truck. However, as the paper progresses, the monster truck idea is not developed, and it is unclear what the special item might be. The organization lacks logic, and there is no coherence to the piece. There are enough errors and consistent violations in standard English grammar, usage, and mechanics to distract the reader and make the writing difficult to read.

The Language of Writing Assessments

Providing students with the language used in evaluating what they read can carry over into how they are able to talk about and assess their own writing. The qualities that make for effective reading are directly connected to techniques used by writers. The following are some vocabulary terms that are useful in conversations about writing.

- Coherence: *The Literacy Dictionary* (Harris & Hodges, 1995, p. 38) defines coherence as "the extent to which ideas in text appears to 'hang together' in a clear, unified pattern." Writing assessment rubrics often include this in the descriptor dealing with organization; however, it really deals with a more global view of organization in that it denotes the overall unity of the piece of writing and the consistency with which this unity occurs.
- Conventions: Conventions are accepted standard usages in grammar, punctuation, capitalization, spelling, and paragraphing. This element may be analytically subdivided into distinctive traits or may be holistically scored as one.
- Fluency: The term *fluency* has various meanings. In reading, it is defined as accuracy in decoding, automaticity in word recognition, and appropriate use of prosodic features and juncture (Pressley, 1998). However, in writing assessments fluency sometimes is connected with writing freely in a continuous stream with many things to say during a free-write, and other times it

is connected with providing fluent and varied sentence structures within a text. Of course, fluency with English language learners' writing usually refers to their ability with a second language.

- Five-Paragraph Essay: This structured writing follows a prescribed organizational pattern that provides a thesis statement with three supporting subtopics in the opening paragraph. This is followed by three paragraphs, all similar in format in that they give details or examples about each subtopic with three or more supporting sentences. The last paragraph provides a summary statement of the thesis and the subtopics. Transitional words, phrases, or sentences are used to tie the paragraphs together. It is especially useful in convergent writing tasks. The inherent danger in this structured format is that it can result in formulaic, stilted writing, which is not generally valued in divergent writing situations.

- Graphic Organizers: These visual representations can be in an outline or pictorial form and are used as a way to gather and organize information. They are most often used in the prewriting and revision processes for composing or reorganizing a piece of writing.

- Idea or Focus: Students need time to reflect on a topic, focus and define what they would like to say, and then draft initial writing from which they can continue the process of writing and revising. Assessment criteria may include rewards for originality or risk taking.

- Organization: This defines the logical, orderly plan of idea development in a piece of writing. Some recognized organizational patterns include chronology, spatial, cause-effect, compare-contrast, process order, climactic, or problem-solution.

- Style: Style is generally defined as an author's unique way of conveying his or her writing, with a view toward audience and purpose. It may include literary strategies (e.g., analogies, illustrations, examples, anecdotes, figurative language, repetition) to clarify a point or develop a main idea. Precise and varied word choices and analytical, evaluative, and creative thinking often define the style of an individual piece of writing.

- Syntax or Sentence Variety: These terms refer to the grammatical patterns in which sentences are formed and the ways they influence the rhythm and sound of the language in the piece of writing. Varied forms are valued in most writing assessment criteria.

- Thesis statement: This is a sentence or longer statement that identifies the main point being addressed in the piece of writing. In formal, structured writing, it begins the writing by stating the argument or premise on which the rest of the piece is based.

- Transitions: These organizational words, phrases, and sentences are used to connect ideas to one another. They are often tied to the purpose of the piece of writing.

Rubrics

A rubric is a set of graduated performance levels of proficiency based on descriptive criteria that explain the important elements of the work being evaluated at each level. They are used as scoring guides through which student samples and progress may be assessed based on established proficiency criteria.

Qualities of performance are described on a rating scale and may or may not also include point values. Standards of excellence are described in developmental degrees of mastery through descriptions of student work or products. They can be used before writing to provide students with expectations for assignments and also used after writing to measure student proficiency and progress.

At the level of large-scale assessments, rubrics can be used to consistently evaluate student papers. At the classroom level, these same rubrics can be used to help students self-assess and revise their writing.

Standardized Rubrics

The scoring guide used by the NAEP program has six-point standardized rubrics for each type of writing that is assessed: narrative, informative, and persuasive. The scoring guide describes student responses as (6) excellent, (5) skillful, (4) sufficient, (3) uneven, (2) insufficient, or (1) unsatisfactory. The use of even-numbered rubrics allows evaluation of upper- and lower-end papers and is often used in proficiency examinations designed to report achievement levels. For more information, visit the NAEP Web site (http://nces.ed.gov/nationsreportcard/writing/).

The Northwest Regional Educational Laboratory uses a five-point standardized rubric for its 6+1 Trait writing assessments. They provide descriptors for scores of five, three, and one and use the even numbers for writing that falls between the odd numbers and that may contain elements of each. They focus on the traits of ideas, organization, voice, word choice, sentence fluency, conventions, and presentation. For more information, go to http://www.nwrel.org.

Teacher- and Class-Designed Rubrics

Rubrics designed to measure processes and those developed to measure products differ. Multiple steps in a process approach necessitate rubrics for work on subsequent drafts, whereas product-focused rubrics merely define and describe elements of single pieces of writing. Teachers and students can design rubrics together by analyzing sample papers and listing the features that seem to work well with the type of writing being created and assessed. These may be done after writing as part of the initial assignment directions or as part of the prewriting and revision portions of a process-based writing approach.

Steps involved in designing classroom rubrics include the following:

1. Identify the task and the key elements involved in completing the task. This can be done in a whole class discussion or developed in small groups and then shared with the whole class.

2. Determine the gradation levels of proficiency and assign them labels. If appropriate, assign point values such as (6) superior or exemplary, (5) above average or very good, (4) acceptable or adequate, (3) in need of improvement or emerging, (2) poor or nonproficient, and (1) indecipherable written response. (A blank paper would receive a zero.)

3. Sort the sample papers within each of the defined levels. In the absence of sample papers, teachers and students might interactively write samples they believe will best illustrate the different levels.

4. Using the sorted papers, teachers and students work together to discuss and describe the key elements that define each level.

5. In groups or individually, have students write a rubric using the descriptors.

6. Field test the rubrics with the assignment and decide how useful it is in evaluating the writing.

In designing rubrics, students become more thoughtful evaluators of the quality of their own and others' work. In addition, the rubrics help provide diagnostic information in a practical format to allow students to improve their own work in an independent and responsible manner.

Checklists

Checklists usually are used at the classroom level to guide the peer-review process, a teacher-student conference, or individual revision or editing. Depending on the goal, checklists can be tightly focused or extensive in terms of guiding revision processes.

Short checklists can be mastered and combined into larger units once the skills are familiarized through frequent usage. They can be formatted as checklists such as Tables 2.6 and 2.7, or they can indicate levels of adequacy, as in Table 2.8. Note that in the checklists provided for each case, one is focused on the process and the other on the product. Both require teacher and student attention for development in proficient writing.

WRITING ASSESSMENT FORMATS

Today's eighth-grade English class starts off like any other. Myiesha looks up from her mirror and smiles serenely at her arriving friends, Krishon and Deborah, as she gives one last check to her hair, makeup, and general appearance. Just then, Anthony and George push their way into to the classroom together, crowding their way simultaneously through the single doorway as they catcall across the room to Joe. All three girls roll their eyes in utter disgust at the boys' immature antics. Then the bell rings.

"Okay, class," announces Mrs. Williams. "Your peer-writing assignments are on the board. Get your papers ready and proceed to your assigned partners to fix your papers. Hurry up now. Who hasn't gotten with their partners yet? Joe, you're with Krishon. Deborah, you're with George. And Myiesha, you team up with Anthony today."

"Um, Mrs. Williams?" ventures Deborah. "I think today is my day for teacher conference."

"And I was supposed to work on my prewrite because I was absent yesterday," offers Krishon.

"Well, okay. Then George and Joe, you work together. Now, everyone get busy," Mrs. Williams orders.

Myiesha cannot believe her bad luck. She is now faced with sharing a very personal piece of writing with Anthony, class blabbermouth. She quickly sifts through her writing folder to find something—anything else—to share.

Table 2.6   Checklist Examples for Student Review

Process-Focused Personal Checklist for Writing

_____ I have included all my prewriting notes and drafts with this assignment along with my written observations on how my thinking and drafts progressed. See *notes to myself* attached.

_____ I have checked to make sure my ideas fit the assignment, and I have answered the question completely. See *notes to myself* attached.

_____ I have included the three introductions I tried with this piece and the reasons why I chose the one I did for the final copy.

_____ I have included the two conclusions I tried with this piece and the reasons why I chose the one I did for the final copy.

_____ I read my paper aloud to myself, and I like the way it all sounded.

Product-Focused Personal Checklist for Writing

_____ I have my name and the date on my paper.

_____ I answered the question thoroughly.

_____ All my sentences show a complete thought.

_____ Each of my sentences continues the thought from the previous one and supports my main idea.

_____ I used transitions well between my sentences and paragraphs.

_____ I chose specific words to describe and show action.

_____ I began all sentences with capital letters and checked for ending punctuation.

_____ I indented all new paragraphs.

_____ I checked the spelling of all words that I was not positive I knew.

_____ I read it aloud to someone, and he or she helped me with the grammar and usage.

Table 2.7   Checklist Examples for Primary Student Review

Process-Focused Personal Checklist for Primary Writing

Yes	No	Not sure	Indicator
			I am turning in all my prewriting and revised drafts.
			I can tell you why this writing is important to me.
			I can explain the reasons why I told things in this order.
			I can show you where I used good details or examples.
			I read my paper out loud and changed any parts that needed fixing.
			I think I am finished with this paper for right now.
Here's what I think I'm going to work on next:			

Product-Focused Personal Checklist for Primary Writing

Yes	No	Not sure	Indicator
			I followed the directions.
			All my ideas fit together.
			I have a beginning, middle, and end.
			I chose interesting and appropriate words that my readers will like.
			All my sentences are complete.
			I checked all my words for spelling mistakes.
			I checked all my capitalization and punctuation.
			I like the way my paper sounds when I read it out loud.

Table 2.8   Checklist Examples for Peer-Response and Teacher-Student Conferencing

			Process-Focused Peer-Response or Teacher-Conference Checklist
Absent	*Present*	*Strong*	*Indicator*
			There is evidence of prewriting in initial notes and drafts.
			Each draft shows progression of writer's craft.
			The ideas are clear, insightful, and consistent throughout; the focus becomes clearer with each draft.
			In reading it aloud and through discussion, it is evident that the writer has made substantive changes and genuine revision.
			Attached *notes to myself* show thoughtful reflection and evaluation.

			Product-Focused Peer-Response or Teacher-Conference Checklist
Absent	*Present*	*Strong*	*Indicator*
			Idea, Focus, and Content
			The writing responds completely to the assignment.
			The focus is clearly evident.
			The main idea is developed with relevant, important ideas and details.
			Examples and support all relate to the central focus.
			Design and Organization
			A recognizable order guides the reader through the text.
			An appealing introduction opens the writing.
			A satisfying conclusion ends the writing.
			Transition words and phrases move the piece along.

Table 2.8 (Continued)

			Product-Focused Peer-Response or Teacher-Conference Checklist
Absent	*Present*	*Strong*	*Indicator*
			Language, Style, and Voice
			Appropriate diction and precise vocabulary are used.
			Language and style reflect an understanding of audience and purpose.
			Sentence Fluency, Syntax, and Structure
			The piece of writing exhibits a variety of fluent, rhythmic sentence patterns.
			Sentences are complete (no fragments), and there are no run-on sentences.
			Standard Conventions
			Capitalization and ending punctuation are all correct.
			Internal punctuation is correct.
			Spelling is correct.
			Paragraphs are correctly indented at appropriate sections.
			Grammar and usage are correct.

ASSESSING PROCESSES

Peer Assessment

After much practice with teacher conferencing and self-assessment, peer assessments can be one of the most valuable tools for a writing classroom because they help writers to share thinking about a piece of writing. This type of conference requires a classroom climate of trust and much teacher modeling before students are able to assist one another in significant ways. In the preceding scenario, Myiesha evidently has a piece of writing that requires a specific partner, and she is correct in choosing another piece of writing. With a preset protocol, she could also explain her problem to Mrs. Williams, who could reassign her to another, more appropriate partner.

We begin introducing peer reviews with a think-aloud dialogue, using a piece of our own writing, and two voices, one for the responder and one for the writer. For example,

Writer: Hey, I just finished this piece of writing. Do you have a minute to listen to it?

Responder: Sure. Just a sec. I have to finish this one sentence on my own piece first.

Pause

Responder: Okay. I'm ready.

Writer: This is about a time I had to go to the store for my mother and didn't have the right amount of money.

Responder: So go ahead and read. I'm listening.

From the two-voice dialogue model, we move to use of the *Author's Chair*, a strategy in which a student sits in front of the classroom and shares a piece of writing he or she has read or written. Using this approach, we can practice response techniques publicly with authentic writing. As the writer reads the piece aloud, the listener can simply pay attention to the story and respond by retelling or summarizing the essence of the piece and describing the parts he or she likes best, or the reader and writer can guide their conference with a checklist of questions that can be used for discussion. The items on the peer-response checklist will vary depending on the focus of recent instruction, or, in the case of convergent writing, it will depend on the rubric or instructional emphasis placed on the assignment.

The final evaluation portion of a peer conference is determining how well the peer-review conference went and how productive it was for the writer and the responder in developing their literacy skills. Valid feedback and constructive suggestions for improvement usually are more helpful than mere quantitative scores or grades. In addition, both the writer and the responder should evaluate the process to determine how best to use it in the future.

Groups of students can also work in peer conferencing situations, using discussion to assist one another in practicing the craft of revision and to develop literacy through interaction. As in any group discussion process, whether for literary or informational reading or for peer response in writing, the goals and protocols of the group must be established before successful peer response can be accomplished. Much modeling and careful attention to group dynamics are a necessary part of teacher preparation in this structure. Some help with positive and useful responses is necessary, certainly at first. Because this type of assessment is based on conversation, every event is different.

The Teacher-Student Writing Conference

The writing conference can be another means of assessment designed to evaluate and support students' progress in writing. Through brief check-in chats about students' current progress along the way to completion of the assignment, teachers can assess development and engagement with the assignment or piece of work and can also intervene in any potential or real problems that are bothering the student. By focusing on students' personal writing concerns (e.g., "What difficulties did you have while writing this?" or "How did you think of ways to tell about this?"), the teacher emphasizes the process and the meaning students are trying to convey.

This conferencing time can provide important opportunities for assessing students' instructional needs and for encouraging oral discussion in sorting out problems and directing plans for future development of the piece of writing. This can include assistance in narrowing the focus of a topic, adding important details, and motivating the student to continue crafting the piece of writing or moving on to the publication stage. Certainly, the primary focus of each conference must be on the student's message, as reflected in the piece of writing. What the student is saying is of primary importance, and helping him or her decide how to say it is the secondary but also vitally important assessment task of the conference.

For convergent writing tasks, the initial conference actually begins when the assignment is made. At that point, the student should have the opportunity to discuss the purpose of the assignment and the teacher's expectations. This may be a good time to introduce an evaluative rubric and previous student samples, indicating the range of possible responses to the topic.

The teacher-student writing conference is also an opportune time to model effective peer-conferencing strategies. It takes much practice to become proficient at conferencing. Active listening skills and helpful questioning techniques become more effective with greater familiarity with the author's work and with a focus on what the writer is trying to say. We often start by asking how the piece of writing is going, or we ask about the topic the student has chosen. See Table 2.9 for a checklist on conferencing writers.

Self-Assessment

The writing conference is the means by which teachers move students to self-editing independence. After practicing with a checklist and editing tools

Table 2.9 Assessing Your Skill at Conferencing Writers

Do you listen actively, with genuine interest?

Do you begin by focusing on what the writer has to say?

Do you attend to specifics of the piece of writing rather than generally on the writer?

Are you able to identify what the writer has done well with this piece of writing and tell him or her about it?

Do you have a common writers' vocabulary that can help you and the writer communicate about the writing?

After a conference, are writers motivated to keep writing, take chances with new techniques, and continue working on their writing?

with teacher assistance, students are encouraged to practice self-talk, based on the teacher-student talk of initial editing conferences. They need to practice moving between the roles of "involved writer and detached critic" (Calkins, 1986, p. 119). Later, by describing the approaches taken individually, teachers can reinforce student efforts at self-assessment in thinking about a piece of writing, examining possible revisions, and acting on them.

Having students write possible discussion questions to assist in group work and personal learning is one of the most concrete ways to connect assessment and learning activities. Student study groups are an effective means for preparing for quizzes or tests and a way for them to take control of their own learning. In addition, students can respond to self-evaluation questions they have in their own process. See the form provided in Table 2.10.

Table 2.10   Self-Assessment Inventory

Name _____	
Date _____	
Title of paper _____	
Here's what I did well on this paper.	Here's what I plan to work on.

ASSESSING PRODUCTS

One of the most effective ways of teaching students how to self-assess their own work is to model self-evaluation of a writing task. Sharing a teacher-written piece of writing and thinking aloud about the ways in which an experienced writer revises and edits a piece of writing is the best way to begin to help students assess their own writing pieces.

In addition to conferences focused on processes, editing conferences are a way to assess student knowledge and understanding and to determine possible whole class instruction or review needed conventional usage, punctuation, and spelling lessons. The editing conference provides practice and modeling for students in the use of editing tools and in developing self-editing procedures for a piece of writing that is ready for publication. In the earliest grades, rather than sending students back to their seats to look up misspelled words in the dictionary, working in small groups and practicing ways of using dictionaries to spell and define words is more effective. Later, whole class or small group instruction on word processing programs with spell- and grammar-check features are also better scaffolded with teacher and peer support. Editing checklists and practice with dictionary and spell-check usage can begin as teacher-directed activities and lead to independent practice. Checklists progress from basic conventional issues such as capitalization and ending punctuation in the early grades to longer and more advanced lists of spelling, grammar, usage, and mechanics, as seen in Table 2.11.

Moving editing and writing conferences from teacher directed to student centered is valuable in helping students assume responsibility for their own written work and become self-sufficient writers.

Holistic Scoring

Focused holistic scoring is based on the notion that a piece of writing, like any other work of art, is worth more than the sum of its individual parts. Evaluation by trained scorers is determined through a general overall impression of the text based on comprehensive quality. Topic treatment, rhetorical methods, word choice, and conventional usage are all considered as contributing to a relative total effect. Scaled rubrics with defined categories are given corresponding point values, and exemplary models, known as anchor papers or benchmarks, are provided to represent each score. For each scoring session, readers undergo training updates with a review of the rubric and benchmark papers to calibrate for consistent scoring. See Table 2.12 for an example of a holistic scoring rubric. The advantage in holistic scoring is the speed of scoring and, with reliable training and scoring procedures, the validity of the assessment in determining proficiency for the writing assignment.

Primary-Trait Scoring

In primary-trait scoring, a form of holistic scoring, a single feature is considered for evaluation based on a specific task. It can range from individual features connected to specific writing forms, such as persuasive writing, to the single trait of idea development in content areas. It is the basis of most constructed-response item writing that involves content areas in reading, math, science, and social studies. The trait under consideration in this type of convergent writing is

(Text continues on page 51)

Table 2.11   50 Possible Mini-Lessons for Sequential Editing Checklist Tasks

1. Capitalization: student's first name

2. Sentence recognition and development

3. Capitalization: first word in sentence

4. Punctuation: period

5. Punctuation: question mark

6. Usage: subject-verb agreement

7. Capitalization: names of people and places

8. Usage: some verb forms

9. Dictionary skills

10. Double negatives

11. Capitalization: *I*

12. Usage: *a* or *an* before a vowel

13. Usage: *I* coming second in compound subject

14. Capitalization: months and days of week

15. Punctuation: abbreviation of months and days

16. Punctuation: comma in complete dates

17. Punctuation: comma in letter salutation

18. Punctuation: comma in letter closing

19. Capitalization and abbreviations: *St., Ave., Dr.*

20. Capitalization: titles of stories, books, movies

21. Punctuation: series comma in lists

22. Contractions, using apostrophes: *they're, you're*

23. Punctuation: colon in writing time of day

24. Punctuation: exclamation mark

25. Correct usage of homophones: *to, too,* and *two; their* and *there*

26. Punctuation: hyphen to separate syllables at the end of a line

27. Punctuation: apostrophe for possession

28. Paragraphing as new idea or change in direction

29. Punctuation: quotation marks

30. Punctuation: comma before or after quotation marks

31. Capitalization: first word of quotation

32. Paragraphing with new speaker or quotation

33. Punctuation: comma usage in combining simple sentences

34. Usage: *me* coming second as the object

35. Punctuation: colon for listings

36. Punctuation: comma usage in appositives

37. Run-on sentences

38. Punctuation: semicolon

39. Punctuation: commas for groups of words in a series

40. Fragments

41. Punctuation: comma usage in complex sentences

42. Usage: pronoun–antecedent agreement

43. Usage: verb tense agreement

44. Capitalization: proper adjectives

45. Usage: correct pronoun case

46. Punctuation: comma to set off interrupting word or expression

47. Usage: correct adverb or adjective as modifier

48. Parallel construction

49. Passive voice

50. Common word confusions depending on student usage, e.g., *accept* vs. *except*, *affect* vs. *effect*, *less* vs. *fewer*, *lie* vs. *lay*, *whose* vs. *who's*

Table 2.12   Holistic Scoring Rubric

This paper is
6: Outstanding in every way.
Ideas are developed in a compelling, insightful manner. Focus is well controlled, with precise and relevant details or evidence, and organized in a clear, coherent manner to showcase the central idea or theme. The paper demonstrates the author's unique style and provides a strong sense of audience and purpose. Varied sentence length and structure enhance the stylistic effect. This paper has few if any errors in standard conventions in grammar, usage, and mechanics.
5: Very good and distinctly above average.
Ideas are effectively developed with details or evidence. Focus is defined with clear and coherent organizational structures. Style reflects a sense of commitment to the topic, audience, and purpose. Uses varied sentence length and structure effectively. The paper has few errors in standard conventions in grammar, usage, and mechanics.
4: Adequate and meets the assignment requirements.
Ideas are presented in a satisfactory manner, with adequate details or evidence. Focus is evident and organized in an acceptable manner. Style is appropriate to audience and purpose, and organization is suitable. Sentence length and structure are sufficiently varied but may be predictable. Although some errors in standard conventions may be evident, they do not distract the reader or indicate a basic misunderstanding of conventional use.
*****
3: Slightly deficient and does not meet the assignment requirements.
Ideas are present but may not be developed with details or evidence. Focus is attempted or may fade in and out. Minimal organization may interfere or provide irrelevant information or digressions. There is an absence of understanding of appropriate style suited to audience and purpose. Sentence length and structure are limited or rambling. The paper has some noticeable flaws in standard conventions that indicate some basic misunderstanding of conventional use.
2: Weak and needs much revision and editing.
Ideas, when present, lack focus and development, with little or no detail or evidence. There are serious problems with organizational structure and coherence. The paper fails to engage the audience appropriately, and the purpose is confusing. Sentences may be very simplistic or run on, with no link to one another. The paper has serious flaws in standard conventions that confuse the reader with discrepancies.
1: Very weak and needs extensive revision and editing.
Ideas are jumbled, and there is no clear focus. Details and evidence, when present, are confusing and not connected to a main idea. Little or no organizational structure is evident, and there appears to be no sense of audience or purpose. Sentences may be incomplete, with little evidence of sentence sense. The paper contains an overwhelming number of errors in standard conventions, making the paper, in some cases, indecipherable.

relevant idea development based on the content of the answer; that is, how well the writer has succeeded in accomplishing the task associated with the item. The scoring guide for this type of writing generally includes a copy of the writing topic, expected criteria for student responses, an explanation outlining the connection between the primary trait and the task, a rubric of point scores, and annotated samples of student papers (Lloyd-Jones, 1977).

Multiple-Trait Scoring

Like primary-trait scoring, multiple-trait scoring is criterion based. In this case, however, more than one trait is evaluated for proficiency. In a constructed response item in math, for instance, computation and problem-solving steps might receive separate scores. In writing evaluation, traits of writing such as ideas, organization, vocabulary, sentence usage, grammar, and mechanics are separately analyzed for effective treatment. Analytic trait-rating scales are established with elements of effective writing as determined by national, state, or local standards and used in scoring student papers. Its distinct advantage over holistic scoring results is the diagnostic information it provides for students. See Table 2.1 (on page 20) for an example of a multiple-trait analytic scoring rubric as adapted from NAEP criteria.

ORGANIZING AND ADMINISTERING YOUR OWN SCORING SESSION

Finding What You Value

State standards provide a guide to the criteria that should be emphasized in state and district writing assessments. They often include familiar criteria such as well-developed ideas and information, well-organized writing with clear transitions, a variety of appropriate word choice and sentence structures, and control over grammar, spelling, and punctuation usage. Persuasive writing rubrics additionally focus on the importance of being able to take a clear position that the writer can support with well-chosen details, reasons, or examples. They also address the importance of clear organizational frameworks, specific word choice, varied sentence structures, and few errors in spelling, grammar, and punctuation.

Classroom teachers may determine which qualities of writing are important to assessment at the current point of instruction and can focus on them as primary or multiple traits in designing rubrics and prompts. Doing this in collaboration with students makes this a worthwhile instructional exercise for all the language arts (i.e., listening, speaking, viewing, reading, and writing).

Choosing the Prompt and Rubric

Perhaps the most important part of the entire assessment process is beginning with a well-developed writing prompt or assignment and allowing some discussion of its intent. A good question is clear, addresses the content being assessed, is of interest to students, and is feasible to answer in the time and space allowed. Students need to understand what they are being asked to produce and why. They should understand not only the purpose of the assignment but also the format and criteria on which it will be evaluated. The prompt and rubric should be field tested with real students and teachers to determine their effectiveness and to discover any problems they might present to both readers and writers.

Selecting Exemplars

By using models of student writing at all levels of proficiency, students have an example of what is expected, and scorers can better understand the criteria for evaluation. To ensure reliability in large-scale assessments, anchor papers are selected from large numbers of student papers. After quickly reading and sorting randomly selected papers into high-, medium-, and low-quality piles, experienced lead readers choose appropriate anchor papers for each score. Consensus on their suitability is then decided by the lead readers and the table leaders, who will assist in the scoring session. Training packets of rubrics and anchor papers are compiled for each reader to use in the scheduled training and scoring session.

At the classroom level, students can help in sorting through anonymous papers to choose high-, medium-, and low-quality papers and to discuss their reasons for assigning the point values. We have predetermined papers and never use our own current students' papers in this process, although we do occasionally borrow from some students' writing to create a composite paper that best exemplifies points we will discuss.

Scoring and Discussing

Each scoring session begins with a review of the writing prompt, the rubric, and the anchor papers. Scorers practice with anchor papers to define group standards on which to score. Consistency in scoring is facilitated through the effective writing criteria defined in the rubric and sample anchor papers. Anchor papers are used in the initial training and are also reviewed after any pause in scoring for rest breaks or lunch. Table leaders and lead readers provide second scores to check for consistency in scoring. Inconsistently scored papers receive additional readings.

At the classroom level, we use the scoring and discussion period for students to self-evaluate their work. We also use this time to provide them with opportunities to revise and edit their work before turning it in for a final teacher evaluation.

Next Steps for Instruction

When scoring thousands of papers at the state level, we do not have the same opportunities that we have at the school level. As we finish scoring a grade-level set of papers at a school site, if site-based teachers are scoring, we ask them to include a small note to each student, thanking them for sharing their writing and pointing out what they liked most about the content. Children love receiving these notes, especially from former or possibly future teachers.

FINAL THOUGHTS

Assessment is not a substitute for writing instruction. It is a way of guiding instruction to provide meaningful teaching and learning activities. Computer-generated data based on readability formulas with vocabulary features, syntax, sentence length, and word counts do not provide the necessary information to identify effective discourse. For that is what writing is: an expressive means of discourse.

Use of rubrics and checklists to teach writing must allow time to focus on both the process and the product in ensuring excellent writing instruction. By using students' oral and written ideas on how and why they are making choices as writers, we can help them develop their writing craft and their thinking.

Writing assessments need not be used solely for the purposes of outside evaluation and policy decisions. Site-based scoring sessions and student-led evaluation procedures, using descriptive criteria and process-oriented discussions, can provide some of the most powerful means of helping young writers. Even with quantitative tools such as rubrics, point systems, and field-tested prompts, writing assessment is not an exact science. However, it does provide some basis for assisting teachers and students in their thinking and composing processes.

REFERENCES

Calkins, L. M. (1986). *The art of teaching writing.* Portsmouth, NH: Heinemann.

Graves, D. H. (1983). *Writing: Teachers and children at work.* Portsmouth, NH: Heinemann.

Greenwald, E. A., Persky, H. R., Campbell, J. R., & Mazzeo, J. (1999). *The NAEP 1998 writing report card for the nation and the states.* Washington, DC: U.S. Department of Education, Office of Educational Research and Improvement, and National Center for Education Statistics.

Harris, T. L., & Hodges, R. E. (Eds.). (1995). *The literacy dictionary: The vocabulary of reading and writing.* Newark, DE: International Reading Association.

Hosic, J. F., & Hooper, C. R. (1916). *A child's composition book.* Chicago: Rand McNally.

Hosic, J. F., & Hooper, C. R. (1932). *American language series: Book two.* New York: Rand McNally.

Johnston, P. H. (1984). Assessment in reading. In P. D. Pearson (Ed.), *Handbook of reading research* (pp. 147–182). New York: Longman.

Lloyd-Jones, R. (1977). Primary trait scoring. In C. R. Cooper & L. Odell (Eds.), *Evaluating writing: Describing, measuring, judging* (pp. 33–68). Urbana, IL: National Council of Teachers of English.

McFadden, E. B. (1912). *A course of study in the teaching of composition, language, and spelling for the first three years* (teachers' ed.). Sacramento, CA: Superintendent of State Printing.

Myers, M. (1980). *A procedure for writing assessment and holistic scoring.* Urbana, IL: National Council of Teachers of English.

Noyes, E. C. (1912). Progress in standardizing the measurement of composition. *English Journal, 1*(9), 532–536.

Parker, R. G. (1833). *Progressive exercises in English composition* (3rd ed.). Boston: Lincoln and Edmands. Edition also available online at http://digital.library.pitt .edu/cgi-bin/t/text/text-idx?c=nietz&view=toc&idno=00abh4625m

Pressley, M. (1998). *Reading instruction that works: The case for balanced teaching.* New York: Guilford.

Thorndike, E. L. (1911). A scale for measuring the merit of English writing. *Science, 33*(859), 935–938.

White, E. M. (1994). *Teaching and assessing writing: Recent advances in understanding, evaluating, and improving student performance* (2nd ed.). San Francisco: Jossey-Bass.

Wolcott, W., & Legg, S. M. (1998). *An overview of writing assessment: Theory, research, and practice.* Urbana, IL: National Council of Teachers of English.

Reading Assessment

Ruth and Caren, two teachers at an urban elementary school, met before the school year began to organize their classrooms and curricula. As they worked they chatted about the newly mandated reading assessments at their school.

Ruth: I heard that we have to pick three reading assessments from the assessment list, and we have to administer them during the first few weeks of school.

Caren: I got that memo, too. I am not sure what to give to my kids. All I want to do the first week is get them into a routine. Now I have to do assessments, and I am not sure how long they will take. Do I have to do each kid separately? That could take forever. Which ones are you planning on using?

Ruth: I never taught fourth grade before. I just planned on using our new reading program with everyone. I think it has placement assessments. Why don't we look at those and see what they assess? It looks like we will have to group kids for some of our reading instruction.

Caren: This is really different from what we have done before. I think we may need to have a grade-level meeting and find out what everyone is doing. I think we should all use the same assessments. That way we can compare how our students do throughout the school year. We can check to see what really works with this new program.

Ruth and Caren's conversation can be heard in many elementary schools where teachers are given a choice about assessments. Principals and districts are now expecting teachers to use informal and formal assessment to determine where students are academically at the beginning of the year and throughout the year. Teachers like Caren and Ruth struggle with implementing assessments so early in the year, and they wonder how these assessments will inform their instruction. They are wise in that they envision the changes in their curricula based on the findings of the assessments. They have begun this ongoing conversation and will bring in the whole grade-level team to explore learning and assessment throughout the year.

This chapter explores assessments that teachers can use at the very beginning of the school year to come to know the strengths and needs of their students in reading. These assessments are grouped first for the youngest students in the primary grades and then moving to intermediate grades. When the assessments are grouped this way, it is important for teachers to select the assessments that best fit the students in their classrooms. The primary and intermediate groupings are used just as a format to share assessments, not as a discrete boundary in which primary assessments are appropriate only for students in the primary grades, for instance. Assessments that teachers might use at the beginning of the year, progress monitoring, and diagnostic assessments are explored. Throughout these discussions, formal assessments, typically not designed by teachers, that can be used for progress monitoring or end-of-year outcome measures for school and district accountability are described.

TEACHER-CREATED ASSESSMENTS

This section considers informal assessments that teachers create and use with students in the first weeks of school to discover their strengths and also throughout the year. We place these assessments first because we see teachers choosing from a rich array of practical assessments closely tied to instruction to use in making instructional decisions that are best for their students. Many of these assessments are administered as part of routine instruction so that they do not take up valuable instructional time.

Primary Grades

Language, Sounds, Words, and Book Knowledge

At the beginning of an academic year, primary-grade teachers often are most concerned with oral language, book concepts, and letter knowledge. The following are assessments that target these needs. For primary children who have acquired the following knowledge, teachers will want to consider assessments appearing later in the chapter for intermediate students.

Oral Language and Vocabulary

Children enter school with great variability in vocabulary knowledge (Hart & Risley, 1995). Whitehurst and Lonigan (1998) indicate that children from high-poverty backgrounds typically have fewer experiences with books, writing, hearing stories, and learning and reciting rhymes when they enter school. Although there is always great variability within groups identified by income level, in general, children from lower-income families begin school with fewer literacy experiences and less literacy knowledge, or knowledge about literacy that is valued in school. Importantly, very few children do not partake in literacy experiences in their homes; many parents share oral stories and conversations with their children. Although these experiences are literacy-rich, teachers often do not see them as being as important as picture-book reading and letter knowledge experiences in supporting school success.

The good news is that teachers can make a difference in the school literacy achievement of children from high-poverty backgrounds. Socioeconomic levels demonstrate modest effects on children's later achievement, and effective instruction allows children to progress at rates equivalent to that of children from homes with more financial resources (Goldenberg, 2001), thus showing the importance of the teacher in children's academic lives.

Although there is variability among children, teachers have been assured that primary-level books have vocabulary that is more sophisticated than the daily conversation provided by college-educated parents (Cunningham & Stanovich, 1998). As teachers read and converse with students about books and as they observe children in center activities and on the playground, they make critical observations about children's oral language.

Teachers can identify how a child uses language. For example, does he or she rely on informal language to express ideas, or does the child include academic language? Teachers can look for shifts in language to more academic language. They might hear a child say, "That word sounds like this one. They both end with *at.*" This is a significant difference from an earlier focus on the illustrations in a text in which the children talked only about the pictures and ignored the words. Teachers can also check linguistic knowledge. For example, a teacher can assess a child's syntactic ability by listening to the composition of sentences produced by the child. In these observations, the teacher might record that the child now says "He went" rather than "He goed." Table 3.1 provides a record for teachers' observations of a child's oral language production. Like all provided charts, it can be adapted to each teacher's needs.

As teachers observe closely how students use language in informal and formal learning situations, they discover whether students understand the vocabulary used in stories or informational text. For some students, a quick "This is what this word means" will help them comprehend a text (e.g., "*Dazzling* means *bright*") (Beck, McKeown, & Kucan, 2002). In other situations, particularly with informational text that may have several specific words tied to content, a teacher may want to create a vocabulary chart with picture support or have students participate in a know–want to know–learned (KWL) strategy (Ogle, 1986) to support vocabulary understanding and development (Beck et al., 2002).

A focus on vocabulary is important for young students. Although most teachers do not use formal assessments with students to discover vocabulary knowledge, informal observation of the words students use and understand is important for school success. If teachers introduce a new word with younger students, they can use a strategy such as Word Wizard in which each time a student uses the new word the student puts a check next to his or her name (Beck et al., 2002). Simple strategies such as this one ensure that each child engages in multiple opportunities for practice with the new word or words.

Table 3.1   Assessment of Oral Language

Name _____

Date   _____

Home language

Child relies on home language (this could mean that the child uses a home language that is not the language of the class, such as Spanish) and is unaware that the teacher and other students do not have the background to understand what he or she is communicating. (Example: Child talks about an activity that happened outside school and provides few details. The teacher is assumed to have been there and to understand necessary background.)

Examples

Telegraphic language

Child names objects and people. He or she uses greetings and responses. These responses are brief, and one word often represents a whole sentence (e.g., *there*). The teacher may not understand what the child is trying to communicate because so much of the message is missing.

Examples

Conversational language

Child uses phrases or sentences to communicate. Enough background is provided so that the listener can understand based on this conversation. This conversation is more extended and allows a listener to comprehend.

Examples

Academic language

Child uses academic language in conversations. (Example: Child talks about summaries of stories.)

Examples

Language structure

Child speaks in grammatically correct sentences and uses appropriate vocabulary.

Examples

Teachers record specific language they hear a child using. Teachers may want to include more categories, such as play center, library, or book reading, where they observe language interactions. They may also want to include a category that reflects the new words children use in various activities. For example, when does a child use the word *amazing* after having explored it with the teacher on several occasions?

Name Writing. For kindergartners, their names are the most meaningful words in print and an important first step in literacy (Bloodgood, 1999; Clay, 1975; Lieberman, 1985). Bloodgood observed that when writing their names, three-year-olds used mock letters or scribbles in the fall and were able to correctly represent their first names by spring. Additionally, these children recognized the letters in their names and could read their classmates' names as well. Moreover, as children became competent in writing their names, they began to grasp knowledge of letter names and the alphabet.

Name writing is an assessment of literacy for young children (Table 3.2). Children who are still scribbling their names in kindergarten are not able to represent letters. Children who are starting to use symbols and perhaps their first initials are aware of letters, although they probably are not able to identify the majority of them. And children who are able to represent their names correctly recognize many letters of the alphabet and probably are ready to explore sound-symbol relationships with the first letters of their names as an entry point (Tolchinsky, 2003).

Name writing assessment is easy to complete. Kindergartners just write their names on paper. This paper could be for any assignment, or the teacher could have children write only their names for assessment purposes.

Phonological Awareness. *Phonological awareness* is a broad term that covers children's understanding of the sounds of letters and how they are manipulated within words. For example, children might orally indicate whether the beginning sounds in *bed* and *big* are the same or different. The development of this knowledge is extremely important for young students, for it translates into reading success in later grades (Dickinson & Tabors, 2000; Snow, Burns, & Griffin, 1998).

Within phonological awareness, children must learn to orally

- Identify rhyming words.
- Identify syllables in words.
- Identify onset and rhyme in words (e.g., "bag, b–ag").
- Isolate phonemes in words (e.g., "What is the first sound in *run?*").
- Identify phonemes in words (e.g., "What is the same sound in *fun, fox,* and *fall?*").
- Categorize phonemes (e.g., "Which word is different: *bus, big,* or *fox?*").
- Blend phonemes (e.g., "What word is made when these sounds are put together: *b–i–g?*").
- Segment phonemes (e.g., "How many sounds are in *bug?*").
- Delete phonemes (e.g., "What is *smile* without the *s?*").
- Add phonemes (e.g., "What is *rain* if I add a *t* to the beginning?").

Most teachers can informally assess phonological knowledge during reading instruction. In small groups, a teacher might ask students to orally demonstrate any of the above-mentioned aspects of phonological awareness. Then the teacher records individual student's responses so that further instruction can be targeted to strengths and needs. Table 3.3 provides a record sheet for phonological knowledge. An advantage is that phonological knowledge can be assessed during instruction and does not require a special assessment time.

Table 3.2   Assessment of Name Writing

Name _____

Date _____

_____ Does not differentiate drawing and writing and uses large scribbles for both.

_____ Uses a tight scribble for writing and broad scribbles for drawing.

_____ Uses letter-like forms to represent name.

_____ Uses initial consonant for name.

_____ Represents most letters in name.

_____ Represents first name.

_____ Represents first and last name.

Observations as child writes name.

(Teacher might want to tape an example of name writing for later comparison to this chart.)

Table 3.3   Assessment of Phonological Knowledge

Name _____

Date _____

Identify rhyming words.

Identify syllables in words.

Identify onset and rhyme in words (e.g., "*bag: b–ag*").

Isolate phonemes in words (e.g., "What is the first sound in *run?*").

Identify phonemes in words (e.g., "What is the same sound in *fun, fox,* and *fall?*").

Categorize phonemes (e.g., "Which word is different: *bus, big,* or *fox?*").

Blend phonemes (e.g., "What word is made when these sounds are put together: (*b–i–g?*").

Segment phonemes (e.g., "How many sounds are in *bug?*").

Deletion of phonemes (e.g., "What is *smile* without the *s?*").

Addition of phonemes (e.g., "What is *rain* if I add a *t* to the beginning?").

In core reading programs and in the intervention program *Road to the Code* (Blachman, Ball, Black, & Tangel, 2000), there are specific activities that facilitate phonological awareness assessments. For example, teachers might engage students in an activity called *Say It and Move It.* Students are asked to move a tile when they hear a sound. At first this activity reveals how many sounds a student hears. Following success with identifying the number of phonemes, students move tiles for each phoneme that is heard using a left-to-right structure. If the teacher says *man,* the student would move three tiles to represent each phoneme. Activities such as this one make the assessment process enjoyable for students, and assessment occurs simultaneously with teaching.

Alphabet Knowledge. Similar to phonological knowledge, alphabet knowledge is important for young students (Adams, 1990). Students use this knowledge to recognize and decode words. Alphabet knowledge is broken up into letter recognition and sound-symbol relationships.

- **Alphabet letter recognition.** Teachers can assess this knowledge by having a student identify uppercase and lowercase letters. All the teacher needs is a chart with the alphabet printed on it, although the letters should not be in a specific order because children may have memorized them this way. Often teachers explore a child's knowledge of uppercase letters first, then lowercase letters, and then a mixture of both.

To see whether children can represent letters, a teacher just needs to ask students to write various letters. In Figures 3.1 and 3.2, two attempts to write

Figure 3.1 Alphabet Knowledge

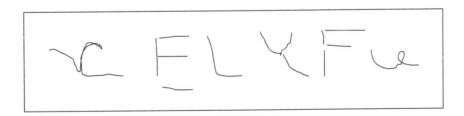

Figure 3.2 Alphabet Knowledge

letters are shared. In the first example, Gabriel is representing letters in a conventional way. All of his attempts are at capital letters, which is not unusual for beginning writers. Importantly, his attempts are close approximations of the letters he is writing. His representation of letters is more sophisticated than scribbles used by children before they are aware of letter representations or before they have the fine motor coordination needed to create letters on paper. With more knowledge of the alphabet, the child whose work is shown in Figure 3.2 easily recorded both uppercase and lowercase letters. In this example, the child was able to represent capital and lowercase letters easily.

- **Sound-symbol knowledge.** Once children become familiar with the alphabet and the names of letters, teachers need to assess their knowledge of sound-symbol relationships. Teachers can do this orally by asking individual children, or they can assess this in small groups in which children write the beginning sound of a word. Teachers can also learn about a child's ability to map sound and spelling during an informal spelling assessment discussed later in this chapter.

Concepts of Print. Clay (1972) developed an assessment, *Concepts About Print Test*, which targets many aspects of books. Her test assessed children's knowledge of concepts such as book orientation (front and back); difference between illustrations and print; directionality of print; book terminology such as *word, letter, top and bottom of a page;* and the beginning and end of a book. Clay used specific books that she developed for this assessment, and teachers can use simple, predictable text to learn about a child's knowledge of a book and print.

This assessment must be done with one child at a time, and often teachers enlist the help of a parent or aide to accomplish this assessment. A teacher would select a simple, predictable text that has a title page. Once the book is selected and the child is sitting next to the teacher, the teacher completes the following steps for this assessment.

- **Book orientation.** Present the book upside down or backwards to the child. Say, "Show me the front of this book. Can you show me the title of the book?" If the child points to the title, the teacher asks, "What is the purpose of the title?"

- **Differences between illustrations and print.** The teacher opens the book to the first page. Then he or she asks a child to point to the illustrations and then to the print. If the child is able to do this, the teacher has the student point to the place where you should start reading.

- **Directionality of print.** The child points to the first line of text. Then the teacher asks how you should read this print. The child makes a sweep from the left to the right under this line. If the child can do this, then the teacher asks where you would read the next line, looking to see whether the child again moves to the left.

- **Beginning and end.** The child points to the beginning and end of the book.

- **Book terminology.** The child is asked to point to the top and bottom of a page. Then he or she is asked to point to a word. If the child can do this, then he or she is asked to point to a specific word. If the child can do this, then he or she is asked to point to a letter in the word. A teacher might also see whether the child recognizes uppercase and lowercase. After this exploration, a teacher asks questions about punctuation.

This information provides teachers with evidence of children's experiences with books. For children who have little experience, teachers will need to explicitly help them develop this knowledge. Table 3.4 shares an assessment record that can be used in classrooms for book and print knowledge.

- **Concept of Word.** Most young children do not understand how words are represented in print. In oral language, one word merges into another. However, in print, spaces separate one word from another (Tolchinsky, 2003). Children who are able to point to words as they read or who point to words as their teacher reads have more sophisticated knowledge of reading, writing, and spelling. In fact, they are considered to be beginning readers (Morris, 1980, 1993).

To assess this concept, children need to learn a short poem or nursery rhyme. In this poem or rhyme there must be one or more two-syllable words. A poem that works easily for young students is "One, two, buckle my shoe." Once the children know the poem orally, the teacher meets with one student at a time. The following is the process to assess concept of word.

Share a written copy of the poem with the child. If there is time, the teacher can write the poem as he or she says the words.

1. Teacher reads the poem, pointing to each word.

2. Teacher reads the poem with the child, together pointing to each word.

3. The child reads the poem, pointing to each word.

4. Teacher asks the child to identify individual words such as *buckle, shoe, shut,* and *three.*

As the child reads, the teacher marks on a copy of the poem the reading behaviors of the child. The following are typical results and what they mean for instruction:

- **No concept of word.** The child moves his or her finger under words randomly. If a child correctly points to a word, it is by chance. When asked to identify specific words, this child usually just points anywhere. This child needs support in learning the alphabet and having the teacher model finger pointing during reading. It will be difficult for this student to identify words or initial or final letters because he or she is unsure of where a word begins or ends in print.

- **Rudimentary concept of word.** This child understands that there is one word for each syllable; he or she is using a one-to-one strategy. Once this child gets to *buckle,* trouble begins as the child points to *buckle* for *buck-* and to *my* for *-kle.* The child may self-correct at the end of the line. If this child gets stuck when reading, typically he or she needs to return to the beginning and

Table 3.4   Assessment of Book and Print Knowledge

Name _____

Date _____

Book orientation

_____Able to point to front and back of book

_____Able to point to title

_____Able to identify purpose of title

Differences between illustrations and print

_____Able to point to illustrations

_____Able to point to print

_____Able to point to where reading of a book should begin

Directionality of print

_____Able to show directionality of print on a page

_____Able to show return sweep of print

Knowledge of beginning and end

_____Able to point to beginning of the story

_____Able to point to end of the story

_____Able to point to beginning of text on a page

_____Able to point to end of text on a page

Uses book terminology

_____Able to identify top and bottom of a page

_____Able to point to a word

_____Able to point to a specific word

_____Able to point to a letter

_____Able to point to a specific letter

_____Able to point to lowercase letter

_____Able to point to uppercase letter

_____Able to identify a period

_____Able to identify a question mark

_____Able to identify an exclamation mark

Notes:

start once again. When asked to identify individual words, this child will return to the beginning of the poem to find each word. This child has a beginning understanding of how words are recorded in print and with support can work on sound-symbol relationships in words.

- **Full concept of word.** Students with full concept of word can easily read and point to words. They are not tricked by two-syllable words. They are easily able to identify individual words and do not need to return to the beginning of the poem to do this. These students are considered beginning readers, and they have an understanding of sound-symbol relationships.

Table 3.5 is a form for documenting student's concept of word. This assessment is more labor intensive than other beginning-of-the-year assessments. However, it yields valuable information about students and their initial reading strengths. Once this assessment is completed individually, it can be observed during instruction and does not require one-on-one assessment again. All a teacher needs to do is have children point to the words they are reading during a guided reading time.

Decoding

Teachers often evaluate the decoding accuracy of young students. They know that it is important for students to be able to independently decode words because this ability supports reading development (Pressley, 2006). To assess this ability, they often engage students in running record assessments as they work with a small group of students. Teachers ask all students in their reading group to reread familiar text, and as students are engaged in this process, they target one student to listen to carefully. Running records often become a routine part of small group work during reading instruction.

A running record is conducted by having a student orally read a section of text (Clay, 1993). Teachers often use leveled readers for this assessment. Many schools have determined appropriate levels for grade-level expectations. For example, a Reading Recovery level of 16 often is earmarked for end-of-first-grade achievement. Importantly, the teacher listens carefully to the fluency of reading and any oral miscues a student makes. The teacher records these diversions from text to determine strategies that a student uses for deciphering unknown words. For example, a student may say *house* when *horse* is on the page. The student is using the initial consonant and other letters in the word for this miscue. If the student corrects this substitution because meaning is impaired, then the student understands that meaning is important. If the student continues reading, then the teacher knows that the student's goal is to get to the end of the passage, with meaning not considered important. These two patterns result in different instructional decisions by the teacher. For one child, the teacher will focus on decoding alone; for the other child, the teacher will focus on decoding and gaining meaning.

In preparation for a running record, teachers often photocopy the section of text they expect students to read. They are then able to mark on this text any diversions from text a student produces. Other teachers use blank paper and record checkmarks for each word read correctly. When a student deviates from text during reading, these miscues are reported on the paper. In using either

Table 3.5   Concept of Word in Print Assessment

Name _____

Date _____

One, two, buckle my shoe.

Three, four, shut the door.

Buckle _____

Shoe   _____

Shut   _____

Three _____

Results

_____ Full concept of word

_____ Rudimentary concept of word

_____ No concept of word

(Teachers mark where the child points and what the child says. So if the child says-*kle* and points to *my*, the teacher would indicate-*kle* above *my*. If this is corrected, the teacher would note the correction. Typically, children have only the short poem in front of them. This sheet is for recording the child's reading behaviors.)

format, the goal is to determine the strengths and needs of students as they orally read text. This written record allows a teacher to determine strategies that a student is using to decode unknown words. Typically, running records are more focused on oral reading than comprehension, although teachers can create questions to determine a student's understanding of text. Table 3.6 shows a running record sheet completed by a third-grade teacher. The notes at the bottom are the teacher's interpretation of the miscues the student made. These observations will be used during instruction for this student. Table 3.7 shows a running record in which the teacher used checkmarks.

Although teachers usually use text that is marked with a level, either Reading Recovery, Lexile, or grade level, they do not have to rely on this information to be provided to determine a level. The following are two ways in which a reading level can be determined.

A sample of text is typed into Microsoft Word. Using Microsoft Word on a PC, go to the *Tools* menu and click *Options,* then click the *Spelling and Grammar* tab. Select the *Show Readability Statistics.* Click OK. On the *Tools* menu, click *Spelling and Grammar.* Then it will display information about the reading level from a variety of formulas. On a Mac, go to *Spelling and Grammar* on the *Tools* bar and then click on *Options.*

Use one of the readability formulas easily available on the Internet. Commonly available formulas include Fry, Smog, Dale-Chall, Flesch, and Spache. Each formula has specific instructions to follow for a sample or multiple samples of text.

Comprehension

There are several ways in which teachers can evaluate primary students' comprehension. The following are several strategies that can be implemented during classroom instructional time. These strategies offer ways to assess reading comprehension of younger students and are also applicable for assessment of comprehension in later grades.

Retellings. Retellings are an informal assessment of comprehension (Gambrell, 1996). Retelling can be aided or unaided. In unaided retellings a reader is asked to remember details from the passage or book he or she just read. A teacher can write what a student says or tape record the retelling of the student. The teacher does not prompt for recall. In aided retellings, the teacher might ask, "Were there other characters? What happened? How did the story end?"

Before asking a student to retell a story that he or she read, the teacher should make an outline of the characters, plot, setting, and so on. In this way, the teacher can check off when a student provides this information.

To evaluate a retelling, a teacher might use a rubric. The following is one possibility for a rubric:

- The student does not recall the major elements of the story even with prompting.
- The student identifies characters, setting, problem, and solution with prompting. The information is sketchy.

Table 3.6   Running Record

Name <u>Anthony</u>

Date <u>September 9</u>

(Selection from Bourgeois, P. (1993). *Franklin is bossy*. New York: Scholastic.
Reading Level 2nd grade, Lexile Level 290, Reading Recovery Level 18)

There was no one to play with and nothing [note/never] much to do. So, he helped his father [dad] all afternoon. They weeded [worked] the garden and washed the floors. And they made supper [dinner] for Mole because he was sick.

"You're a good friend," Mole told Franklin's father. [fa/dad]

On the way home, Franklin asked, "Do you and Mole have fights?"

"Sometimes," said Franklin's father. "But we always make up."

NOTES: Anthony read with some fluency. He read in phrases rather than word by word. He used the initial consonant as a clue when he did not know a word (e.g., *note* and *never* for *nothing*, *worked* for *weeded*). He kept working at a word when it did not make sense (e.g., *nothing*). His substitution of *dad* for *father* and *dinner* for *supper* did not disrupt meaning, and he did not seem bothered by these substitutions. This text was not difficult for him and is certainly at an instructional level, perhaps independent.

Table 3.7   Running Record

Name _____

Date _____

(Selection from Minarik, E. (1957). *Little Bear.* New York: Harper and Row. Reading Recovery Level 19)

Text	Running Record				
It is cold.	√	√	√		
See the snow.	√	√	√		
See the snow come down.	√	√	√	√	here/down
Little Bear said, "Mother Bear,	√	√	√	mo/mother/sc	√
I am cold.	√	√	√		
See the snow.	√	√	√		
I want something to put on.	√	√	some/something/some/T		
	√	√	√		

NOTE: *sc* = student corrected; *T* = teacher told child the word.

- The student identifies characters, setting, problem, and solution with minimal prompting. Events are in the correct sequence.
- The student identifies characters, setting, problem, and solution with no prompting. Events are in the correct sequence, with rich description.

Retellings allow a teacher to discover the depth of a student's comprehension. Although they take time to administer, they provide information on which aspects of text a student is paying attention to. They can also provide a window into the inferential understandings that a student gleans from text.

Drawing and Writing. After reading, students are asked to draw and then write about their drawing. As students mature in their writing ability, this activity can just be writing without a supporting illustration or quick sketch. Teachers need to be mindful of the drawing as part of this assessment. It should not be an art project but rather a quick sketch to support writing. This activity can be very teacher directed or open ended. A teacher may just ask students to draw and write about the part of the story they remember best. In this way, teachers learn about which aspects of the story or informational text were best remembered.

From such an open response, teachers can narrow what they expect students to do. The following are several expectations that teachers can provide students for assessment purposes. This is just a brief sample to provide ideas for teachers to use as they create their assessments for comprehension.

- Narrative text, focused on content
  - Draw and write about the main characters. What did you learn about them in reading the story?

- Draw and write about the events that happened at the beginning, middle, and end of the story.
- Draw and write about the setting. How was this setting important to this story?
- Summarize the story.

- Narrative text, focused on comprehension strategy
  - Draw and write about the prediction you made about this story. Draw and write about what happened in the story.
  - Draw and write about the details in this story that helped you understand the main character.
  - Draw and write about three words that were important in understanding this story.

- Informational text, focused on content
  - Draw and write about the _____ that you read about. Include important details.
  - Draw and write about the causes of _____.
  - Draw and write about the timeline shared in _____.
  - Draw and write about the comparison you learned about when reading about _____ and _____.

- Informational text, focused on comprehension strategy
  - Draw and write about the strategy you used to understand this text.
  - Draw and write about the important words that you learned about in this text.
  - Draw and write the important facts you discovered.

- Functional text (maps, menus, directions, etc.), focused on content
  - Draw and write about what you learned to do in this text.
  - Draw and write about which steps you think were most important.

- Functional text, focused on comprehension strategy
  - Draw and write about which steps were confusing.
  - Draw and write about how you read this text. What did you do first to understand it?

Response Formats. Response formats are very similar to what was shared in the previous section. However, when using response formats, teachers create documents that ask for particular responses from students. For instance, in Table 3.8 a teacher is focusing on several aspects of comprehension that he or she wants to make sure students have acquired. Although each student can respond differently, they are expected to support the answers that they provide, and all questions are very specific. Another format for a narrative text is shared in Table 3.9. In this format, students are expected to compare two characters. After the comparison is complete, students are asked to

Table 3.8   Response Format for Narrative Text

Name _____

Date _____

1. Write a sentence that describes the setting of this story.

2. Choose one character in this story. Use your book to find and record text that describes your character. Find three descriptions of this character.

    1.

    2.

    3.

3. What is the most important event in this story? Explain why you think this.

4. Describe how you felt as you read this story. Did you agree with the way the characters behaved? Why do you think this?

Table 3.9   Character Comparison

Name _____

Date _____

Choose two main characters from your story. At the top of the paper, write how they are alike. In the middle of the paper, write how they are different. At the bottom of the paper, write what is most important to know about each character.

Write Names of Characters

_____   _____

Alike

Different

What is most important about

_____   _____

synthesize this information and choose the most critical characteristic of the character.

Informational text lends itself to response formats. Teachers often mirror the structure of the informational text. So if the text is written in a descriptive format, students are expected to provide details of the description. If another format is used, the expectations would vary and match the text's structure. Common organizations of informational text are descriptive, cause and effect, timeline, comparison, and problem–solution. Functional text often is organized in a sequence, as evidenced in directions. See Figure 3.3 for common structuring of response formats for informational text.

When teachers use these formats, they are expecting convergent responses from students. For instance, if students are comparing frogs and toads, there would be a fixed list of comparisons based on the details that were read in the text. These formats provide a very specific structure to determine comprehension of text.

Intermediate Grades

Word-Level Knowledge

In most cases, teachers of intermediate students are most interested in whether their new students can read grade-level material and how fluent they are in this process. They need to know quickly which students are below grade level so they can adjust their grade-level material and perhaps provide reading interventions.

Developmental Spelling Assessment

The goal of a developmental spelling assessment is to determine a student's knowledge of English orthography, or how students represent the sounds and meaning patterns in words. This knowledge often translates into reading proficiency. Students who are able to represent only single-syllable, short-vowel words are considered beginning readers. Students who are experimenting or can represent single-syllable, long-vowel words are more fluent and can read longer texts. Students who are experimenting and can represent multisyllabic words tend to be proficient readers.

One way to gain this knowledge is to study several writing examples produced by a student and determine how this student represents words. A more efficient way is to ask students to spell certain words that are ranked by familiarity (how often they appear in books) and difficulty (consonant-vowel-consonant words to multisyllabic). This assessment is similar to a spelling test in which a teacher says a word and uses it in a sentence, and then students write it as well as they can. Table 3.10 is a list of words that are often used with students (Bear & Barone, 1989). Resources such as *Words Their Way* (Bear, Invernizzi, Templeton, & Johnston, 2004) and *Word Journeys* (Ganske, 2000) provide numerous word lists and activities for students.

A teacher can discover the following information from this assessment:

- Ability to represent initial and final consonants (e.g., *b, d, c, p*)
- Ability to represent short vowels in single-syllable words (e.g., *bed, ship*)
- Ability to represent blends (e.g., *dr, cl, tr*)

Figure 3.3   Informational Text Response Formats

Descriptive 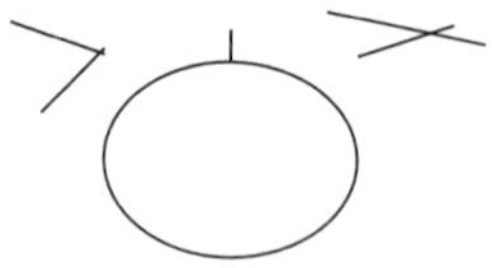	Cluster
Cause and Effect	Cause Effect
Timeline	Insert Dates and Describe Events
Comparison 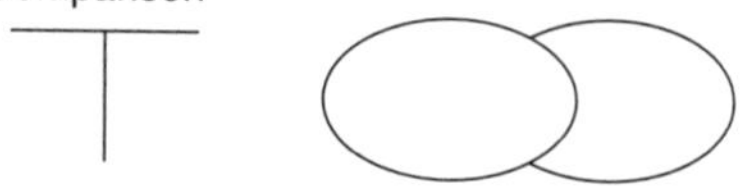	T chart or Venn Diagram
Problem–Solution	T chart Problem Solution

Table 3.10   Qualitative Spelling Inventory

Name _____

Date _____

Instructions: Say the word once. Use it in a sentence. Ask the child to spell the word.

If the child misses more than three of the first five words, stop the process. Check this again after 10 words, then 15 words.

Bed

Ship

Drive

Bump

When

Train

Closet

Chase

Float

Beaches

Preparing

Popping

Cattle

Caught

Inspection

Puncture

Cellar

Pleasure

Squirrel

Fortunate

NOTE: Once a child has completed this inventory, check to see what the child can do in representing words (e.g., represent initial and final consonants correctly, represent short vowels correctly).

- Ability to represent digraphs (e.g., *sh, wh*)
- Ability to represent long vowels in single-syllable words (e.g., *drive, train*)
- Ability to represent the addition of suffixes (e.g., *preparing, popping*)
- Ability to represent correct vowel for schwa sound (e.g., *bed*)
- Ability to represent spelling pattern even when sound changes (e.g., *pleasure* from *please*)

Students who are unable to represent initial or final consonants need support from teachers in all reading and writing activities because these students are not very phonologically aware. Students who represent initial and final consonants have awareness of sound-symbol relationships. Students who represent short-vowel words with full phonological representation, for example, *bed* or *bad* for *bed*—are beginning readers and have the concept of word in print. Students who represent long vowels in single-syllable words by using two letters are further along in their understanding of words in that they know that two letters can represent a single sound. They are also more fluent as readers and writers. As students represent more of these words accurately, they are also more proficient as readers and writers.

Although there are no fixed expectations for a student's spelling development by grade level, there are patterns representing the most prevalent spelling development demonstrated by students. Kindergartners through first graders typically are learning to represent initial and final consonants, blends, digraphs, and short vowels. Second and third graders work on long vowel patterns and how to add affixes to words. Fourth graders and beyond move from a consideration of sound and its representation to patterns, as seen in the shift in the word *please* to *pleasure* (Bear et al., 2004).

Vocabulary

Vocabulary knowledge gains importance in the intermediate grades as many concepts in books move from concrete, familiar situations such as family and school to more abstract concepts, especially in content-area studies such as science and social studies. Interestingly, many books centered on vocabulary are organized around teaching strategies rather than assessment (e.g., Baumann & Kame'enui, 2004; Beck et al., 2002; Marzano, 2004).

One of the central problems in direct instruction to increase student vocabulary is that there are too many words to teach directly (Beck et al., 2002). Teachers need to select the most important words, such as the words most critical to a text's central meaning.

Assessing students' vocabulary knowledge happens in most cases during instructional events. For instance, a student is reading in a small group with the teacher, and it becomes clear that comprehension is being impeded by the lack of vocabulary knowledge. In many cases, teachers are proactive and provide activities to build student vocabulary before a comprehension break occurs.

For instance, they could have students scan text and note any possibly confusing words. Students could then partner to discover their meanings and share them with the class or group. Marzano and Pickering (2005) recommend that teachers group vocabulary by subject area, and students learn these discipline-specific words. Several core reading programs build vocabulary by themes, and then texts organized into these themes repeat and extend this core vocabulary. In this way students have multiple opportunities to explore a core list of words so that they become familiar with them.

Bear and colleagues (2004) recommend that intermediate students explore words by meaning, considering roots or bases to extend their vocabulary knowledge. In these situations students might explore words with the root *bene* in them to generate the meaning of this root across words. The words they generate might include *benefit, beneficial, benevolent,* and *benefactor.*

Teachers who want a more systematic way to learn about students' vocabulary as measured against grade-level expectations can target the vocabulary portion of an Informal Reading Inventory (IRI). At the end of each IRI passage there are comprehension questions. Several of these questions are tied to vocabulary. If a student consistently misses these questions, then targeted vocabulary instruction would benefit this student.

Other ways to assess vocabulary knowledge are through the use of activities that expect students to explain word meanings. For example, at the beginning of a text, a teacher may ask students to indicate their level of knowledge of words important to the text (Beck et al., 2002). Table 3.11 presents such a form. After reading, the teacher can ask students to revisit this form and provide examples of each word from text and in their own sentences.

Beck et al. (2002, p. 84) also suggest that teachers can create multiple-choice formats to check on understanding. For instance, for the word *focus* the following choices can be created.

Focus

> To make more clear
>
> To bother by staring at
>
> To look at dreamily
>
> To use glasses for reading

Other suggestions to evaluate students' knowledge about words include the following:

Descriptions: Describe someone who is *humble.*

Relationships between words: How are *solitary* and *aloof* alike and different?

Continuum of words: Arrange words from the least to the most: *massive, miniscule, vast, least, small, gigantic.*

Continuum of words, variation: How much energy does it take to

> Meander down the hall?
>
> Jump over a chair?
>
> Be a spectator in a crowd?

Rank from most to least.

This is just a small sample of the ways in which teachers can determine students' knowledge of important vocabulary. Although they serve as assessment activities, they would also support instruction targeted at vocabulary growth.

Table 3.11 Vocabulary Assessment

Name _____

Date _____

Word	Know It and Can Explain It	Know Something About It	Have Seen It Before	Don't Know the Word
Exceptional				
Wondrous				

Comprehension

Core Program Assessments. In core reading programs, placement tests and assessments are used throughout to determine a student's progress. Teachers can use these assessments to determine the success of a student in comprehending the text that has been taught directly during reading instruction. Many core programs have separate booklets, with a full range of comprehension and other targeted reading areas available.

Response Formats. These were discussed in the comprehension assessments for primary students. They certainly fit here as well. They can be used to target specific comprehension information provided by students about the texts they read.

Dialogue Journals. Dialogue journals allow students to write reactions, feelings, or questions about what they have read. These written responses provide a window into a student's comprehension of text. Barone (1990) found that students often retold text or summarized it when they were still trying to figure out what was happening in the plot. They moved to inferential responses when text reading became easy and they understood the literal elements. Tables 3.12 and 3.13 show responses written by intermediate students. Table 3.12 is a literal response and Table 3.13 is inferential, with personal and text-based inferences; both were written to the book *From the Mixed-Up Files of Mrs. Basil E. Frankweiler* (Konigsburg, 1967). This book is centered on a brother and sister who run away to the Metropolitan Museum in New York.

Instructionally, dialogue journal entries can be used as a forum for serious discussions about books because they can be the stimulus for deeper conversation about text. They can also be used for assessment because they allow a teacher to observe a student's comprehension of text.

Assessing Reading Strategies. Along with content, teachers work with students to develop strategies that they use to understand text. Teachers can assess the strategies that students use through discussion (e.g., "How did you figure out this section of text?"). They can also engage students in a reading conference in which they discuss the content and the processes used during

Table 3.12   Literal Dialogue Journal Entry

Claudia didn't regret bringing Jamie along because he had a transistor radio. She appointed him treasurer and he had to keep track of all of the money. He tried to get her to change her mind and go to Central Park but she said, "They might get mugged or robbed or kidnapped."

Table 3.13   Inferential Dialogue Journal Entry

Claudia said, "You had to blab it out blabbermouth." That makes me think of how I say something that I'm not supposed to and I blab it out and everyone calls me a blabbermouth. I hate being called a blabbermouth.

reading. Another way to gather this information is through a chart in which students describe the strategies they have used. See Table 3.14 for an example of a strategy chart.

Fluency

With intermediate students, teachers often are concerned with fluency and target ongoing assessments to discover whether students are improving in this area. They know that if students are very slow paced with reading, comprehension is difficult (Barone, Hardman, & Taylor, 2006). They also know that students will find the act of reading tedious and laborious and will find it difficult to complete reading assignments. Teachers select a passage of about 100 words that is at a student's instructional level. The student repeatedly reads this passage until he or she can read it at 100 words per minute with no miscues. Teachers often have students do this with a partner, and each student charts his or her progress (McKenna & Stahl, 2003). Table 3.15 provides a record sheet for students to use.

Hasbrouck and Tindal (1992) conducted a study of students in Grades 2 to 5 to determine benchmarks for fluency. For second graders, the rate is expected to be about 95 to 125 words per minute by spring. For third graders, the rate is expected to be about 115 to 145 words per minute by spring. For fourth graders, the rate is expected to be about 120 to 145 words per minute by spring. And for fifth graders, the rate is expected to be about 130 to 150 words per minute by spring.

COMMERCIAL ASSESSMENTS

With the advent of No Child Left Behind and Reading First legislation, many elementary schools are using standardized screening and diagnostic assessments in the primary grades so that they can measure growth of students in reading throughout the year. These instruments typically are used three or four times in an academic year.

Early Literacy Knowledge

• Dynamic Indicators of Basic Early Literacy Skills (DIBELS) are a set of standardized, individually administered measures of early literacy development. They are designed to be short (1-minute) fluency measures used to regularly monitor the development of early literacy and early reading skills. The measures were developed to assess student development of phonological awareness, alphabetic understanding, accuracy and fluency reading connected text, vocabulary, and comprehension. Information on DIBELS is available at http://dibels.uoregon.edu. The full assessment can be downloaded at this site. Just hit the *Measures* tab for free testing materials.

• **Phonological Awareness Literacy Screening** (PALS) can be used with children in preschool to Grade 3 to identify students at risk of reading difficulties. PALS is designed to measure young children's knowledge of important literacy fundamentals and can be used as a diagnostic tool to provide teachers with explicit information to help guide their teaching. There is variation in

Table 3.14   Strategy Chart

| Name _____ |
| Date _____ |

Describe how you used the strategy.

Before Reading	*During Reading*	*After Reading*
I previewed the text before I began reading.	I reread when I was confused.	I checked back on what I read and summarized it.
I thought about what I know about this text before I began to read.	I thought of new questions that guided me through the text.	I reread sections that were still confusing.
I checked all the bold headings and words before I began to read.	I put ideas together to make sense of what I read.	I thought about how I felt about what I read.
I predicted what might happen in the text.	I used context to figure out an unknown word.	I thought about similar experiences that I have had or similar books I have read.

Table 3.15 Fluency Record

Name _____

Date _____

150														
140														
130														
120														
110														
100														
90														
80														
70														
60														
50														
40														
30														
20														
10														
	1	2	3	4	5	6	7	8	9	10	11	12	13	14

Mark the time you begin reading on a paper. When you finish reading, mark the time. Determine how long it took you to read the passage. Put an X in the square that shows your speed. The 1 is for the first time you read the passage, the 2 is for the second time, and so on. You can try this passage up to 14 times to get your speed to 100 words per minute.

forms for different grade levels, but typically students are asked to spell words, identify words in isolation, orally read and answer comprehension questions, and identify letters and their sounds, and there are phonemic awareness assessments. Information on PALS is available at http://pals.virginia.edu.

- **Texas Primary Reading Inventory** (TPRI) provides a comprehensive overview of students' reading and language arts development. It is designed to be used with students in kindergarten through third grade. A quick screening section works with a more detailed inventory section to help teachers identify strengths and problem areas and monitor progress. It measures phonemic awareness, phonics, comprehension, fluency, and vocabulary. It identifies students who have achieved benchmark scores and those who may be at risk for reading difficulty. Information about TPRI is available at http://www.tpri.org.

Often schools use DIBELS or a similar assessment in the first few weeks of school. If primary students are assessed in an at-risk category, teachers will then administer assessments such as PALS or the TPRI, which are more labor intensive and time consuming, to determine which areas are difficult for a student. These assessments target what instruction will best support a student's current understandings of sound-symbol relationships, for example, and provide guidance for teachers to nudge students to more complex knowledge.

Informal Reading Inventories

Teachers are concerned about students' ability to read and comprehend grade-level text. In intermediate grades, teachers often rely on an IRI to gain this information. Table 3.16 lists several commercial IRIs. For additional information, visit http://www.sedl.org for specific details about numerous IRIs.

IRIs help teachers discover the independent, instructional, and frustration reading levels of students (Betts, 1957).

- **Independent level.** This is the level where a student can read easily and comfortably. The student is accurate and comprehends. Typically the student has fewer than 3 reading errors in 100 words of text and more than 90% comprehension if questions are asked. The student needs no support from the teacher.
- **Instructional level.** This is the level where a student reads with good accuracy and moderate fluency. Comprehension is adequate. Typically, the student has fewer than 5 reading errors in 100 words and about 70% comprehension if questions are asked. Support from a teacher or partner helps this student read more fluently and achieve better comprehension.
- **Frustration level.** This is the level where the material is too difficult for accurate reading or for comprehension. Typically, students have more than 10 errors in 100 words of text and less than 80% comprehension. Students should not be expected to read at this level other than on a limited basis (e.g., when they are scanning for key information).

Table 3.16 Informal Reading Inventories

Bader, L. (2002). *Reading and language inventory.* Upper Saddle River, NJ: Merrill.

It offers word lists and narrative and informational passages from primer through Grade 9.

Burns, P., & Roe, B. (2002). *Informal reading inventory.* Boston: Houghton Mifflin.

It offers sets of graded word lists and reading selections from preprimer to Grade 12.

Flynt, E., & Cooter, R. Jr. (1993). *Reading inventory for the classroom.* Scottsdale, AZ: Gorsuch Scarisbrick.

It offers sets of graded word lists and reading selections from preprimer to Grade 9. It includes four forms (two narrative and two informational).

Johns, J. (2005). *Basic reading inventory.* Dubuque, IA: Kendall/Hunt.

It offers individually administered informal reading tests (six forms). Form E contains new graded passages ranging from the beginning stages of reading through Grade 8.

Leslie, L., & Caldwell, J. (1995). *Qualitative reading inventory.* New York: HarperCollins.

It offers word lists and graded passages. At each level a teacher can assess background knowledge. There are retelling assessments and comprehension questions.

Woods, M., & Moe, A. (1998). *Analytical reading inventory.* Columbus, OH: Merrill.

It offers K–12 narrative and expository passages.

Determining these levels helps teachers know which students will find grade-level materials to be at their instructional level. If students are found to have an independent level for grade-level materials, a teacher would enrich their instruction. If students are found to be at a frustration level with grade-level materials, accommodations would be necessary, along with intervention strategies to accelerate their reading level.

Most teachers are familiar with commercial IRIs, but they hesitate to use them because they are very labor intensive and typically are given to one student at a time. However, we developed a variation of this method in which all students in a class can participate at the same time. Through whole class administration, a teacher learns which students are at, above, or below grade level in reading. Later, as the teacher has more time and students are comfortable with the routines, the teacher can administer an IRI to students below grade level and then to students who found the grade-level passage to be at their independent level.

The process begins when the teacher selects a grade-level passage from a commercial IRI or from the IRI that is part of the core reading program. The teacher makes copies for each student. The teacher also copies the questions that accompany each passage onto a sheet of paper in which a student can write answers. (Teachers need to be careful with this process because often the answers are printed right beneath the questions.) The teacher passes out the passage, and all students begin reading at the same time. When a student finishes, he or she writes down the time. In this way, the teacher can check on fluency while students silently read the passage. Once a student is done, the teacher removes the passage and gives the student the question sheet. The student then writes answers for each question.

Once all students complete this process, the teacher can determine for whom this passage was at an independent, instructional, or frustration level. Teachers might continue this process by giving students passages at a lower or higher grade level if they find the first passage too difficult or too easy. Through this adaptation, a teacher quickly learns the reading levels of his or her students.

Through this variation, teachers determine the silent reading abilities of their students. They can also determine each student's fluency by considering the time spent reading the passage. (Conversion formulas are available with all IRIs for this purpose.) However, they do not know what strategies students use when they discover an unfamiliar word. Use of this variation allows teachers to hone the IRI process so that they have time to individually assess struggling readers while they simultaneously meet the needs of readers at grade level or above.

Teachers often administer IRIs at the beginning of the year for initial placement of students. To determine growth in reading throughout the year, we have seen teachers administer IRIs midyear and again at the end of the year. Through this process, teachers can determine growth in reading level, fluency, and inferential and literal comprehension, among other reading skills.

Vocabulary and Comprehension

A test that is often used to determine vocabulary knowledge in younger students is the Peabody Picture Vocabulary Test (PPVT–III). This assessment is done with one child at a time. It measures both receptive and expressive vocabulary. Information about this test can be found at http://www.agsnet.com. Often speech and language teachers have this test available.

Several reading tests can be used in the classroom to determine comprehension and vocabulary proficiency. We have listed a few of these easy-to-administer tests here.

- **Gates-MacGinitie Reading Test.** This test has a vocabulary subtest for each grade level (MacGinitie & MacGinitie, 1989). There are also two forms that can be used for pretest and posttest later in the year. It can be administered to a whole class at the same time. Through the use of such a test, a teacher could determine the overall vocabulary knowledge of his or her students, based on grade-level norms. Information about this test can be found at http://www.riverpub.com.

- **Gray Diagnostic Reading Test.** This test assesses reading comprehension, decoding, letter knowledge, concepts about print, vocabulary, and phonological awareness. It is administered to one student at a time. Information about this test is available at http://www.proedinc.com.

- **Gray Oral Reading Test.** In this test, the student orally reads passages while the teacher marks miscues. It assesses comprehension and decoding. Information about this test is available at http://www.proedinc.com.

- **Metropolitan Achievement Tests.** This test measures reading and language comprehension. It has subtests that assess cipher knowledge, vocabulary, and phonological awareness. Information about this test is available at http://PsychCorp.com.

- **STAR Reading Computer-Adaptive Reading Test.** Students take this test individually on the computer. It assesses reading comprehension. It is often used in conjunction with the Accelerated Reader Program. Information about this test is available at http://www.renlearn.com.

ONGOING ASSESSMENTS USED TO MONITOR PROGRESS

Once beginning-of-the-year assessments are completed, teachers are ready to provide differentiated instruction for their students, in which they meet in small groups with students and short, direct, targeted instruction is provided to meet student needs. Throughout the year, teachers want to be assured that students are progressing, and they also want to determine specific areas such as fluency or vocabulary that need additional instruction. Furthermore, they want to identify students who need additional intervention beyond the instruction provided to all students to accelerate their learning.

Teachers usually use the measures described earlier in this chapter. Often they use the theme unit tests in their core programs to document growth throughout the year. In this section, we target some of the teacher-created assessments described before and other assessments that are commercially available.

Fluency

Progress can be monitored through the recurrent use of an assessment tool such as DIBELS. Teachers or schools select the subtests they wish to administer to students to determine whether they are meeting grade-level benchmarks. Often they do this three or four times each year. The Oral Reading Fluency subtest often is used for this purpose. For students who are found to be in the at-risk category, this assessment may be given every two weeks to monitor progress, especially if students are receiving a reading intervention in addition to routine reading instruction.

A teacher can also monitor the fluency charts that students are using to document fluency growth. They should see that students move to more advanced levels of material and remain fluent in their reading. They should also note that comprehension is not diminished when reading fluency increases.

Furthermore, teachers can use IRIs as a check for fluency. All they need to do is time a student on the first 100 words of a passage and then check comprehension. In this way they can determine a student's fluency tied to comprehension.

Decoding and Comprehension

Primary teachers often use ongoing running records to determine students' decoding, fluency, and comprehension development. They can easily administer a running record to a student as the remaining students in a small group read independently. This process may be repeated for students on a systematic basis determined by a teacher or school. For example, in the primary grades, running records may be taken every two or three weeks. In the intermediate grades, teachers may determine that every five or six weeks is sufficient.

Intermediate teachers may want to redo the IRI assessment using the variation we described earlier. They may want to use a more advanced, grade-level passage, or they may want to explore how students comprehend using an informational text passage. They probably will reassess their struggling readers to determine whether they are making progress in attaining grade-level expectations.

Spelling

Teachers also reassess students through the use of the developmental spelling inventory. Through this reassessment, teachers can determine whether students have moved to more sophisticated ways to represent words, such as moving from only short-vowel words to long-vowel words, a significant accomplishment for young students.

This assessment provides a window into student growth in spelling. By considering the same words throughout a year, teachers can make careful comparisons to see the new spelling elements that students are using and understanding.

Progress Monitoring Data in Action

We have discovered that in schools that use progress monitoring assessments, the results often are discussed in grade-level meetings. Teachers bring the results from running records or IRIs and discuss and collaborate on students who are having difficulty meeting benchmark goals, for example. Teachers share strategies so that all students are successful. Using data to guide these discussions helps teachers determine which students are making substantial progress and which are struggling. They are able to intervene immediately so that struggling students can make progress, before a long pattern of struggle and frustration is established.

Schools can also use progress monitoring to determine whether there are gaps in their core program instruction. If primary students consistently struggle with phonemic awareness, teachers will want to examine their reading program closely to determine whether this area needs to be shored up. This would be true for all the essential literacy elements.

To help with this examination of core materials, teachers may want to avail themselves of "A Consumer's Guide to Evaluating a Core Reading Program Grades K–3: A Critical Elements Analysis," a questionnaire produced by the University of Oregon (see http://www.opi.state.mt.us/pdf/readingex/consumerguide.pdf). This questionnaire allows teachers to systematically determine how adequately each essential literacy element is taught in each grade. It provides data on the strengths and limitations of their reading program. We used this form with the addition of state and district standards to evaluate a soon-to-be-adopted reading program. With a close look at each year's curriculum, we determined areas that needed to be strengthened before the year began. Although this process was time consuming, it resulted in a much better reading curriculum.

END-OF-YEAR ASSESSMENT

Often at the end of the year, schools and districts are expected to participate in norm-referenced and criterion-referenced tests. These tests are used to determine a school's, district's, or state's performance in reading and other subjects. In Chapter 6, these types of tests are discussed in detail. Importantly, these tests might provide evidence of a broad need for instruction (e.g., students in the school have difficulty with vocabulary), but they do not target instructional needs for specific students. Unlike the other assessments shared in this chapter, these are typically used for accountability, not for instruction.

In addition to these standardized assessments, teachers often engage in one final progress monitoring assessment at the end of the year. Often they use running records, IRIs, or qualitative spelling assessments for this purpose. Through this year-end assessment, they can determine the progress students have made since the beginning of the year. They can discern whether struggling readers made sufficient progress to catch up with their grade-level peers. They can also identify targeted areas of instruction that they can improve next year. For example, if students in general have not made gains in fluency, they can add fluency instruction more systematically to their instruction.

FINAL THOUGHTS

The assessment suggestions shared in this chapter are meant to target instruction to students' strengths and needs. Beginning-of-the-year assessments are critical for students to engage in differentiated instruction. Teachers want to quickly and efficiently provide instruction that results in maximum reading achievement for students. They do not want to frustrate students with instruction that is too difficult, and they do not want to bore students with instruction for content already learned. As the year progresses, teachers want to check in to see that the instruction they are providing results in learning gains. Progress monitoring assessments allow teachers to revise their instruction to meet the more current learning strengths and needs of students. It also lets them target struggling readers to ensure that they get the additional support they need to develop into successful readers. Finally, end-of-year assessments allow teachers to determine the academic growth of each student. They can look at patterns across students to determine whether their instructional program needs changes. They provide opportunities for reflection and refinement of the curriculum.

REFERENCES

Adams, M. (1990). *Beginning to read.* Cambridge: MIT Press.

Barone, D. (1990). The written responses of young children: Beyond comprehension to story understanding. *The New Advocate, 3,* 49–56.

Barone, D., Hardman, D., & Taylor, J. (2006). *Reading first in the classroom.* Boston: Allyn & Bacon.

Baumann, J., & Kame'enui, E. (Eds.). (2004). *Vocabulary instruction: Research to practice.* New York: Guilford.

Bear, D., & Barone, D. (1989). Using children's spelling to group for word study and directed reading in the primary classroom. *Reading Psychology, 10,* 275–292.

Bear, D. R., Invernizzi, M., Templeton, S., & Johnston, F. (2004). *Words their way: Word study for phonics, vocabulary, and spelling instruction* (3rd ed.). Upper Saddle River, NJ: Pearson.

Beck, I., McKeown, M., & Kucan, L. (2002). *Bringing words to life: Robust vocabulary instruction.* New York: Guilford.

Betts, E. (1957). *Foundations of reading instruction.* New York: American Book.

Blachman, B., Ball, E., Black, R., & Tangel, D. (2000). *Road to the code: A phonological awareness program for young children.* Baltimore: Paul H. Brookes.

Bloodgood, J. (1999). What's in a name? Children's name writing and name acquisition. *Reading Research Quarterly, 34,* 342–367.

Clay, M. (1972). *Concepts about print test, sand and stones.* Exeter, NH: Heinemann.

Clay, M. (1975). *What did I write?* Auckland, NZ: Heinemann.

Clay, M. (1993). *An observation survey of early literacy achievement.* Portsmouth, NH: Heinemann.

Cunningham, A., & Stanovich, K. (1998, Spring/Summer). What reading does for the mind. *American Educator,* 8–17.

Dickinson, D., & Tabors, P. (2000). *Early literacy at home and school: The critical role of language development in the preschool years.* Baltimore, MD: Paul H. Brookes.

Gambrell, L. (1996). *Lively discussions! Fostering engaged reading.* Newark, DE: International Reading Association.

Ganske, K. (2000). *Word journeys.* New York: Guilford.

Goldenberg, C. (2001). Making schools work for low-income families in the 21st century. In S. Neuman & D. Dickinson (Eds.), *Handbook of early literacy research* (pp. 211–231). New York: Guilford.

Hart, B., & Risley, T. (1995). *Meaningful differences in the everyday experience of young American children.* Baltimore, MD: Paul H. Brookes.

Hasbrouck, J., & Tindal, G. (1992). Curriculum-based oral reading fluency norms for students in Grades 2 through 5. *Teaching Exceptional Children, 24,* 41–44.

Konigsburg, E. (1967). *From the mixed-up files of Mrs. Basil E. Frankweiler.* New York: Dell.

Lieberman, E. (1985). Name writing and the preschool child. *Dissertation Abstracts International, 46*(12), 3593A.

MacGinitie, W., & MacGinitie, R. (1989). *Gates–MacGinitie Reading Test* (GMRT-3). Boston: Houghton Mifflin.

Marzano, R. (2004). *Building background knowledge for academic achievement.* Alexandria, VA: ASCD.

Marzano, R., & Pickering, D. (2005). *Building academic vocabulary: Teacher's manual.* Alexandria, VA: ASCD.

McKenna, M., & Stahl, S. (2003). *Assessment for reading instruction.* New York: Guilford.

Morris, D. (1980). Beginning readers' concept of word. In E. Henderson & J. Beers (Eds.), *Developmental and cognitive aspects of learning to spell* (pp. 97–111). Newark, DE: International Reading Association.

Morris, D. (1993). The relationship between children's concept of word in text and phoneme awareness in learning to read. A longitudinal study. *Research in the Teaching of English, 27,* 122–154.

Ogle, D. (1986). KWL: A teaching model. *The Reading Teacher, 39,* 564–571.

Pressley, M. (2006). *Reading instruction that works.* New York: Guilford.

Snow, C., Burns, S., & Griffin, P. (1998). *Preventing reading difficulties in young children.* Washington, DC: National Academy Press.

Tolchinsky, L. (2003). *The cradle of culture and what children know about writing and numbers before being taught.* Mahwah, NJ: Erlbaum.

Whitehurst, G., & Lonigan, C. (1998). Child development and emergent literacy. *Child Development, 69,* 848–872.

4

Oral and Visual Assessments

Colonel Francis Parker, one of the most renowned educational leaders and textbook authors of the late nineteenth century, referred to writing as "talking with a pencil" (Parker, 1883/1896, p. 80), and in an early reading text Joshua Leavitt explained, "Reading is talking from a book" (Leavitt, 1823/1847, p. 14). Both Parker and Leavitt were making an effort to combine the literacy activities of reading and writing with speaking and listening. It is easy to see how important oral composition was in curriculum planning in the nineteenth century. With limited access to books and print materials and the lengthy delays associated with written correspondence, oral transmission was the primary means of communication.

Oral composition received much attention in the early twentieth century as well. In fact, numerous educational articles described the importance of a functional curriculum and defended the greater importance of oral rather than written composition because the former had greater application in the world beyond school. Lessons in telephone etiquette and instructions on delivering public readings and speeches are evident throughout language arts textbooks in the first three quarters of the twentieth century. Students were encouraged to speak in large and small groups as part of learning projects in which they often worked in cooperative groups to select, plan, and explore assignments and to present their findings or accomplishments to others.

Recently, however, oracy (listening and speaking) has received less attention than literacy (reading and writing), especially in the focus on standards and high-stakes assessments. The *Standards for the English Language Arts*, a project of the International Reading Association and the National Council of Teachers of English (1996), specifically addresses speaking, listening, and visual arts in several of the 12 standards but only as components of all the language arts. For example, Standard 4 reads, "Students adjust their use of spoken, written, and visual language to communicate effectively with a variety of audiences and for different purposes," and Standard 12 reads, "Students use spoken, written, and visual language to accomplish their own purposes (e.g., for learning, enjoyment, persuasion, and the exchange of information)" (p. 25). We, too, suggest not isolating these skills from the others because they are part of the entire social nature of language and communication. However, we have provided a separate chapter on these language arts to emphasize their importance and to highlight the instructional attention they deserve.

SPEAKING

What do the middle school bully and the bossiest second grader in the school have in common? They can both be terrified at the simple prospect of speaking aloud in front of a class of fellow students. And this doesn't affect just the most fearless schoolchildren. Many adults are brought to their knees at the prospect of presenting ideas and information in a public forum. By providing learning opportunities and assessments in speaking and listening situations, starting in the earliest grades and continuing throughout their school careers, we can better prepare students for the challenges of speaking and listening activities they will experience in later schooling and in life.

Forms of speech at the classroom level can vary depending on the format of discourse and the developmental levels of students. Early childhood speech can take the form of dialogues with adults or other children. They can also occur in monologue playacting with make-believe characters and assumed personas. Through speech, young children negotiate their understanding of situations and meanings. Certainly at the youngest ages, students who talk with a variety of adults who know them well and have sufficient time to share conversations with them will develop mature language at earlier ages (Clay, 1998). It is an important part of children's language growth. As students mature, their speaking skills develop in vocabulary and sentence forms and in longer, meaningful discourse. In the later grades, higher-level thinking skills become critical to the range of thoughtful listening and speaking experiences and assessments as students prepare for more academic conversations.

Speaking activities are closely tied to both reading and writing events. For example, reading aloud fluently is an important measure used in evaluating reading comprehension. (See Chapter 3 for additional information on this subject.) Writing is also closely tied to speaking in that they both deal with creating text. However, unless a speaking event is based on a written text, a speaker does not have the advantage of revising the text before it is heard. In many situations, it is first-draft, spontaneous communication, and ideas are hurriedly constructed and organized based on audience and purpose and delivered in a conventional manner to ensure understanding. Also, with the listener present to provide interactive feedback by questioning, by rephrasing or restating information or by offering clarifying examples, the speaker can ensure that the message is correctly received.

A variety of speaking situations can be provided in addition to normal whole class teacher-led discussions. They may include dialogues aimed at paired decision making and problem solving or a panel discussion of four to seven people to explore issues informally. A symposium of three to six students can present prepared talks on a single subject, or a roundtable discussion can occur in which all students participate as both listeners and speakers. By engaging in speaking and listening activities as individuals and group members, students will gain confidence in speaking situations and experience in dealing with a range of speaking purposes.

Speakers may also have one additional unique challenge. See whether you can recognize it: Circle any of the following effects you may experience before speaking in front of a large group.

1. Shaky hands or cold, sweaty palms

2. Quickened pulse and unsteady knees

3. Trembling lips, dry mouth, and tight throat

4. Loss of appetite or butterfly flutters in stomach

5. Lack of cognitive-processing abilities

If you circled any or all of these items, you have a working definition of *stage fright*. Although some people are apprehensive about reading and writing tasks, it is the act of speaking that holds the greatest fear for the most people. With assistance, students can assess their levels of anxiety, and with instruction they can take appropriate measures to deal with it.

LISTENING

According to the International Listening Association, listening is "the process of receiving, constructing meaning from, and responding to spoken and/or nonverbal messages" (ILA, 1996). In terms of communication, in some ways listeners must be more actively engaged than speakers are in making meaning and connecting new information to existing knowledge. According to researchers, normal speakers speak at around 100 to 150 words per minute (Sticht & James, 1984) and generate about three words per second (Buck, 2001), which allows limited time for those who are listening to process information. This is especially difficult for second-language learners, who need additional time to navigate unknown words, confusing sentence structures, and idiomatic expressions.

For some first-language learners, however, maximum listening rates are about 300 words per minute (Sticht & James, 1984), which allows some time interval after information has been processed. This can offer opportunities for listeners who process quickly to drift mentally to other topics and lose their focus on the speaker's message. In speaking to a diverse audience, it can be difficult to monitor the right delivery tempo to match the needs of those who need a continuous flow of ideas to maintain interest and those who need a slower delivery to process words and information.

Teachers and students need to assess what part of a message, if any, is being received through listener responses to help both the listener and the speaker communicate more effectively. Accurate listening for words, main points, details, and sequencing is an important element in listening proficiency. This is true not just in recounting what has been said but in all areas of comprehension, such as generating predictions, making inferences, drawing conclusions, or looking at concept relationships and styles, which all contribute to better thinking and meaning making.

Perhaps the most important listening skill lessons and assessments are those connected with critical listening skills, such as identifying the importance of certain details, defining propaganda techniques, determining the speaker's purpose and possible biases, evaluating the authenticity of the message, and exploring other potential perspectives that confirm or deny the message. For many years, skillful orators have influenced opinions, swayed values and attitudes, and manipulated the behaviors of a wide citizenry. Just as we teach students the techniques of persuasive speaking and writing, we must also teach them these same techniques from the perspective of critical listeners and readers.

Although listening may be the most relied on language art in terms of the time students devote to its usage, it receives the least amount of instruction. It is often taught incidentally, as part of other curricular activities. According to Moffett and Wagner (1992), one reason oral work gets so little emphasis in the curriculum today may be that it leaves little in the way of an evaluation record. They suggest multiple assessments of students' listening skills, including tape recording students during oral events and keeping a teacher notebook to record firsthand observations of student contributions to discussions and individual oral progress. One method we have found particularly helpful is to use class lists to generate address labels that can then be posted on index cards or a clipboard on which to write comments. These can then be stored in a notebook or file for later review. Another method is to digitally record group discussions to listen to on the ride home from work or later while attending to routine tasks at home. These recordings also can be a means of self-evaluation for students to provide reflection and a record of progress using rubrics and checklists. In addition, when recording group discussions, we use checklists to record group and individual participation. Several of these checklists will be shared later in this chapter.

One particular difficulty in listening is the lack of reflection inherent in its format. Whereas readers can go back and reread for clarity and writers can review and revise, listeners often are expected to comprehend with a single listening event. Although attention is indeed an important aspect, listening well also involves important levels of reasoning and thinking.

WRITING ASSESSMENT FORMATS

Ms. Hartman, who is student teaching in Mrs. Camacho's third-grade class, is working on transitioning her young students from a reading activity to a vocabulary game to prepare them for today's science lesson. "Okay, boys and girls, put your books away and clear your desks so I can give you instructions on a new vocabulary game," she announces.

Jason quickly shuts his book with a pop and shoves it into his desk with a flourish. Others obediently close their books and deposit them in their desks. However, Leonard is still immersed in his silent reading, obviously fascinated with the dinosaur pictures that accompany the text, and several other children are chatting softly to one another with their books open.

"Okay, class. It's time for reading to be over. Put all your things away in your desks so we can move on," repeats Ms. Hartman. She watches patiently as first Joe and then Citrine stop chatting and fumble with their books. Others look up and also close their books and continue to talk among themselves. As she looks toward the back of the room, Mrs. Camacho is smiling, but she points to her watch and rolls her hands to indicate that they need to get going.

"Thank you, Joe and Citrine," Ms. Hartman states purposefully, "for getting ready so quickly." Citrine smiles smugly and turns to her chatty friends and directs them to put their books away and be quiet.

Meanwhile, Leonard is still reading intently. Ms. Hartman walks over to his desk and lowers herself to his eye level. "I'm so glad you love this book, Leonard, but now it's time for our word study game. Would you please put a bookmark in your place and put the book away?"

There probably aren't many teachers who haven't experienced the frustration of orally reminding students to put their names on their papers, take out their homework, or pay attention only to find that after the third reminder, some students have still not managed to comply with the request. When questioned on their inability to hear directions clearly, their response is often something like, "Yes, I heard you, but I guess I wasn't listening."

The problem illustrated here undoubtedly is one of not paying attention as much as it is a problem of not listening. There are a variety of reasons why students' attention can wane during a listening activity. Certainly, background noise, external distractions, or simple daydreaming can interfere. Students' attention is limited, and they tend to discriminate between activities to which they choose to attend. Helping students identify the levels of attention needed for a specific listening task and then helping them increase their levels of concentration to match the task will ensure sufficient attention. Marzano and Arredondo (1986) suggest that athletes and actors are adept at increasing their energy levels to match the task at hand. Some take short breaths, others tense muscles or sit up straight. Helping students analyze their own behaviors can assist them in exploring their most effective listening styles and strategies for personal use. See Table 4.1 for a listening style survey to prompt student reflection and discussion on personal listening preferences.

Assessments can help students determine what behaviors are best suited to increasing their listening levels. The simplest and probably oldest listening assessment used to measure listening skills is Simon Says. The speaker uses sentences that listeners must obey with movement only when the directions are prefaced with the words "Simon says." There are also variations of this type of activity with any set of sounds or gestures cued by specific words. For example, see Table 4.2 for informal primary and intermediate student listening assessments that deal with listening for specific word cues.

Table 4.1 Survey for Listening Strengths

1. When listening to the teacher, I can remember best by hearing the message again in my mind.

Very little like me	A little like me	Pretty much like me	A great deal like me
1	2	3	4

2. The easiest way to solve a problem is to talk about it with someone I know is a good listener, who can give good information and advice.

Very little like me	A little like me	Pretty much like me	A great deal like me
1	2	3	4

3. When I have to remember a phone number or a password and I can't write it down, I repeat the numbers out loud.

Very little like me	A little like me	Pretty much like me	A great deal like me
1	2	3	4

4. When learning a new game, I learn best by listening to someone explain the rules and strategies to me.

Very little like me	A little like me	Pretty much like me	A great deal like me
1	2	3	4

5. When I don't know how to spell a word, I first try sounding it out and writing it by letter sounds.

Very little like me	A little like me	Pretty much like me	A great deal like me
1	2	3	4

6. When I am distracted from my work, it is usually by noises.

Very little like me	A little like me	Pretty much like me	A great deal like me
1	2	3	4

7. When I am solving a difficult math problem, it helps me to talk to someone about it.

Very little like me	A little like me	Pretty much like me	A great deal like me
1	2	3	4

8. When I have to remember a list of items, it is easiest for me to tell myself the list over again out loud.

Very little like me	A little like me	Pretty much like me	A great deal like me
1	2	3	4

9. It is easier for me to follow oral directions than written directions.

Very little like me	A little like me	Pretty much like me	A great deal like me
1	2	3	4

10. I like participating in class and small group discussions.

Very little like me	A little like me	Pretty much like me	A great deal like me
1	2	3	4

Table 4.2a Primary Grade Listening Assessment

Directions: Each time you hear a number, hold up that many fingers in the air.

Five little caterpillars crawling on the floor
One crawled away, and then there were four.

Four little caterpillars heading for the tree
One found a leaf, and then there were three.

Three little caterpillars spinning something new
One blew away, and then there were two.

Two little chrysalises hanging in the sun
One fell down, and then there was one.

One little chrysalis waiting for the day
To become a butterfly and fly far away.

VIEWING AND EXPERIENCING

Most language is associated with nonverbal information, which can supplement or even contradict an oral message. Listening cues, by which a listener offers support to speakers through facial expressions denoting emotions, nodding agreement, or taking notes, are all ways listeners use nonverbal signals to assist speakers in determining the impact of their message.

Speakers, too, use nonverbal cues with facial expressions and hand gestures. Their presentations may also be accompanied by visual representations such as objects, charts, diagrams, maps, demonstrations, or audio and video representations to illustrate a point. "Sharing time," often used in primary classrooms to develop oral language skills, incorporates the presentation of a visual object brought from home that may include a story about the importance of the object or, if it is something created by the student, the process by which it was made. Science teachers also use real objects in an inquiry method to sharpen observation skills and to explain experiments and demonstrations. Social studies teachers, too, have long understood the importance of accompanying their lectures with historical artifacts, maps, and charts.

Sometimes viewing is not accompanied by listening or speaking activities, although these language arts along with reading and writing are involved in responding to all types of viewing events. Wordless picture books, silent film documentaries, artwork, photographs, billboards, and some pictorial charts and graphs are examples of visual experiences that, though not strictly part of the four dominant language arts, are an important element in the art of meaning making associated with their use.

One means of assessing students' visual interpretation skills is to have them view a video without the sound and have them assess the characters' ability to convey the message without audio cues. This can also be done with a speaking engagement in which they hear only the sound, then listen again with the addition of the visual effects to evaluate the more complete message.

Table 4.2b Intermediate Grade Listening Assessment

A Tale From Glitter Gulch

Directions: Divide your students into even groups. Each of these groups will provide the sound effects for one of the items listed below.

The cast reads the story, pausing each time the name of one of the characters or things is mentioned. The group assigned that item calls out the proper sound effect, and the scene continues. At the end of the story when the narrator says, "The end," all the groups call out their various sound effects simultaneously.

Cast	*Sound Effects*
Announcer	Sweet Laurelie: *Sigh*!
Narrator	Dudley Rotten: *Boo*!
Sweet Laurelie	Horatio Hero: *Cheer*
Dudley Rotten	Range cattle: *Mooo*!
Horatio Hero	Coyotes: *Ow, Ow, Owwwwwww*!
Mother	Rattlesnake(s): *Hiss, rattle, hiss, rattle, rattle*!
	Glitter Gulch: *Whoosh! Glitter, glitter, glitter, glitter, glitter.*

Announcer: Ladies and gentlemen, your attention please! You are about to witness a melodrama from the past. You will, as part of the production, contribute to the play by listening carefully and providing the appropriate sound effects for each of the cues.

Narrator: Once upon a time, far far to the west, there lived a poor but lovely girl named Sweet Laurelie. <*Pause*> She and her mother owned a broken-down old place called The Meadows, which didn't make a lot of sense because it was right smack dab in the middle of the desert. It served as a boardinghouse for folks passing through the community of Glitter Gulch, <*Pause*> and that's just what they did sometimes. They passed right through without ever paying their bills.

Sweet Laurelie: Whew! I'm the maid, cook, bell captain, desk clerk, groundskeeper, bookkeeper, and room service all rolled into one! And, boy, am I tired! Or my name isn't Sweet Laurelie! <*Pause*>

Narrator: Dudley Rotten, <*Pause*> the town villain, hoped to marry Sweet Laurelie <*Pause*> and turn the ranch house into a gambling Mecca, right in the middle of the wasteland full of rattlesnakes <*Pause*> and coyotes. <*Pause*> Have you ever heard of such a silly idea?

Dudley Rotten: The mortgage on this poor, rundown old place is due at sundown on Friday! Little do these fools know that I, Dudley Rotten, <*Pause*> have already purchased the mortgage from the bank. Owning the place will give Sweet Laurelie <*Pause*> a good reason to look favorably on my proposal of marriage. That is, if she hopes to keep the place for herself and her mother. A pretty clever scheme, it seems to me, or my name isn't Dudley Rotten! <*Pause*>

Narrator: Meanwhile, our hero, whose name just happens to BE Horatio Hero, <*Pause*> is also hoping to win the hand of the fair Sweet Laurelie. <*Pause*> He works at his no-account mine in Glitter Gulch <*Pause*> and does odd jobs for Sweet Laurelie's <*Pause*> mother, which include running off rattlesnakes <*Pause*> and coyotes <*Pause*> and bringing in the range cattle <*Pause*> at roundup time. As luck would have it, a rich vein of gold running right through his mine has just been discovered.

Horatio Hero: Whoopee! I'm rich! Now I shall be able to ask for Sweet Laurelie's *<Pause>* hand in marriage. We can pay off the mortgage on the boardinghouse and get a little place of our own in Glitter Gulch, *<Pause>* where we can live happily ever after as Mr. and Mrs. Horatio Hero. *<Pause>*

Narrator: As our scene opens, Sweet Laurelie *<Pause>* and her mother are counting the money they have saved in their cookie jar, hoping to have enough to take to the bank to make the mortgage payment tonight.

Laurelie: Oh, mother, what shall we do? We don't have enough to make the payment. Oh, woe is me!

Mother: Never fear, Sweet Laurelie. *<Pause>* Horatio Hero *<Pause>* will surely come up with a plan to save us.

Narrator: Ah, but just now, they are joined by none other than the despicable villain, Dudley Rotten. *<Pause>*

Dudley Rotten: Aha! 'Tis I, Dudley Rotten. *<Pause>* And I have come to collect the mortgage payment.

Mother: Oh, are you working for the bank now, Dudley Rotten? *<Pause>*

Dudley: No, at the moment I hold the deed to this place, and unless you pay up by sundown tonight, the place will be mine, all mine!

Laurelie: Oh, what shall we do?

Dudley: Well, you *could* . . .

Laurelie: Could what?

Dudley: You could marry me. We could run a small but lucrative little gambling business here. At least once we clear out the rattlesnakes *<Pause>* and coyotes. *<Pause>*

Laurelie: Marry you? Never! Not if you were the last man in Glitter Gulch! *<Pause>*

Dudley: Then it's out in the cold with you. You can keep the coyotes *<Pause>* and rattlesnakes *<Pause>* company. I shall return within the hour for your answer.

Narrator: Later that same day, sunset approaches.

Dudley: I am here to foreclose on the mortgage. I want your answer now! Marry me and the riches of Glitter Gulch *<Pause>* will be yours. Turn me down and you'll spend your life dodging rattlesnakes, *<Pause>* listening to coyotes, *<Pause>* and chasing range cattle. *<Pause>*

Horatio: Not so fast, Dudley Rotten! *<Pause>* Unhand her!

Dudley: Curses! It's Horatio Hero! *<Pause>*

Horatio: Dudley Rotten, *<Pause>* you low-bellied rattlesnake! *<Pause>* You cannot have Glitter Gulch *<Pause>* or Sweet Laurelie, *<Pause>* for I have the money to pay the mortgage.

Dudley: Curses! Foiled again!

Narrator: And so, Sweet Laurelie *<Pause>* and Horatio Hero *<Pause>* paid off the mortgage and redid The Meadows into a large, elegant hotel, and Glitter Gulch *<Pause>* flourished amid the rattlesnakes, *<Pause>* range cattle, *<Pause>* and coyotes. *<Pause>*

Laurelie: My Horatio Hero! *<Pause>*

Narrator: The end. *<All sound effects>*

AUDIENCE AND PURPOSE

Although oral language assessments are concerned with form and structure—that is, the sounds of word parts, words, and sentences—they are also an important means of assessing proficient use of discourse to convey and understand meaning. Speaking, listening, and viewing assessments are used for a variety of formal and informal purposes, including paired discussion, small group, large group, and whole class situations.

Audiences

In most situations, just as listeners are evaluating the speaker and the message, speakers are also attempting to assess a listener and modify speech depending on the situation and knowledge of the audience. The challenge with varying audiences is to connect with a diverse group of listeners who may have varying background knowledge, predetermined opinions, and expectations for the topic. Adapting quickly by rearranging ideas, vocabulary, and structure, based on audience feedback, can be difficult as well.

In some whole group situations, speaking can entail a single individual formally transferring or delivering information to an assembly of listeners. In others, such as a town hall meeting, it is designed to generate whole group discussion and to reach a consensus on issues. Robert's Rules of Order were designed to facilitate large group discussions through formal turn-taking protocols. Whereas large groups often negotiate turn taking by raising hands and waiting to be recognized, smaller groups encourage greater personal participation and interaction. In smaller groups and in two-way conversations, there is a greater need for shared responsibility between listeners and speakers to sustain the conversation. Students can share some of the responsibility for evaluating turn taking in group discussions. See Figure 4.1 for a graphic that is adaptable for a teacher or older student to use in tracking small group discussions.

Probably the most common whole class discussions today are those that consist of teacher questions, with students offering answers based on teacher expectations and evaluation of correct responses (Cazden, 1988). Although these activities may provide an informal venue to assess student content knowledge, they are not the best means for assessing students' ability to participate as active speakers and listeners because the structure is mainly teacher dominated. Instead, group discussion assessments can best ascertain students' abilities by evaluating their roles as both active listeners and speakers based on individual and group interactions. This can be accomplished by helping students safely think aloud, search for evidence, make generalizations, and then check those generalizations through additional literacy tasks.

The quality of small group discussions usually is modeled first as a whole group exercise (Smagorinsky & Fly, 1994). For example, before students work in writing-response groups, teachers may demonstrate a variety of modeled discussion procedures for responding to an author's work. Students will observe and react from the different perspectives of responder and author to discover which types of feedback best serve their literacy needs.

Figure 4.1   Small Group Graphic Organizer to Analyze Student Participation

Information can be gathered by the teacher or by another student who acts as nonparticipant observer.

Circles are easily drawn and labeled with participants' names and even positioned where they are sitting in relation to the observer.

Tally marks indicate the number of times a student directs speech to all members of the group. Arrows indicate direction of speech addressed on an individual basis.

As shown in the example below, Kendra and Luis, perhaps unknowingly, seem to be dominating the conversation. John seems to have remained passively silent throughout the discussion.

Example

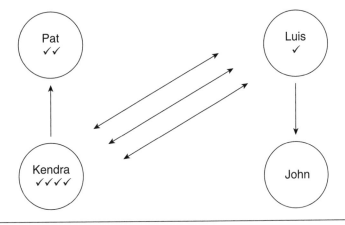

In smaller groups and in pairs, both the listener and speaker continuously are expected to immediately and consistently respond, perhaps without time for reflection or revision as allowed in writing and reading. They need complex thinking skills to respond accurately and relevantly to all situations. Whereas speakers need to check for understanding, listeners also must check when their understanding is incomplete or unclear and decide how to obtain clarification.

Both large groups and small groups can use similar assessment tools to determine effective practice in listening and speaking behaviors. See Table 4.3 for group self-assessment on oral discussions.

Cultural Concerns

Each culture has identified conventions about how conversations should be conducted. One problem in multicultural communities is the varying expectations for discourse that students of diverse home cultures bring to school. As previously mentioned, the most common large or small group discussion forum in the primary grades is "sharing time," in which the whole class or a small group is engaged in listening to an individual student speak. Children often use the familiar style of their families' communities and may sometimes encounter difficulties with the multicultural contexts of a school audience. Eye contact and accompanying gestures differ between cultural communities. If one family believes that children are better seen than heard, those children will come to school with different expectations than those whose parents have encouraged

Table 4.3   Small Group Student Self-Assessment Checklist

____ Topic was clearly defined.

____ Group members stayed on topic.

____ All members listened to others with courtesy and interest.

____ Different points of view were expressed appropriately.

____ Reasons and support were provided for opinions.

____ Questions were used to clarify meaning.

Areas or key points where all members' opinions were the same:

Areas or key points where members' opinions differed:

What did you observe about group members as the discussion progressed?

---

lengthy exchanges. Shirley Brice Heath (1983) discusses differences in socio-cultural contexts for working-class rural communities in the United States and how those differences influence early literacy instruction in school. A pre-assessment survey of language expectations and student interests can help the teacher determine how this factor may influence instructional decisions. See Table 4.4 for student speaking and listening surveys.

Purposes

A variety of purposes have been attributed to speaking and listening assessments. Just as in reading instruction we provide students with a reason for reading and writing, we also need to provide students with reasons for listening and speaking activities. Purposes for listening and speaking assessments often are embedded in other tasks such as topical discussions, problem solving, or learning projects. See Table 4.5 for a chart that summarizes some of the purposes for listening and speaking assessments common to classrooms.

Speakers need evaluation data to improve their skills in organizing and delivering oral messages, both in fluent reading and in oral delivery, in a clear, distinct manner. They need feedback on their abilities to communicate and express ideas, narrate stories, explain information, and provide persuasive discourse. They must also be able to assess their abilities to gather data, solve problems, and develop comprehension skills through speaking and listening experiences.

Listening assessments often are used to monitor correct usage and to determine literal and inferential comprehension levels. Other listening assessments are designed to measure students' ability to relate completeness of thought and to gather comprehensive and accurate information and details. Probably the most important assessments are those that measure students' ability to critically listen to and evaluate information, draw conclusions, and form opinions. The following are purposes for assessing oral and visual language skills, with suggested assessments to measure student progress.

Testing Phonological Levels

Phonological awareness is the simplest of listening assessments. It measures students' ability to differentiate sound segments within speech. Some common assessments have students signal when they hear a letter sound or a rhyme or clap when they hear new syllables in a word. See Chapter 3 for examples of these types of reading and writing early assessments.

Phonemic awareness assessments using listening and speaking skills are appropriate for emergent readers, typically students who are reading at prekindergarten and kindergarten levels. Bringing tacit, subconscious awareness of individual phonemes to the surface is a critical goal of emergent literacy instruction (Bear, Invernizzi, Templeton, & Johnston, 2004). Findings have indicated that instruction and assessments in phonemic awareness do not need to be lengthy to exert the strongest effect on reading and spelling. Because the primary purpose is to help children understand and use the alphabetic system to read and write, research suggests that 5 to 18 hours usually is sufficient, with individual sessions lasting 30 minutes or less (Ehri et al., 2001).

Table 4.4   Speaking and Listening Surveys

Listening Survey

1. What does someone have to do in order to be a good listener?

2. Name your favorite people and places for listening. Why are they your favorites?

3. When you are listening to someone talk in class and you don't understand what they are saying, what do you do? (List all the things you do.)

4. Are you a good listener? How do you know?

5. Would you like to learn how to become a better listener?

Speaking Survey

1. What are some important reasons why people talk?

2. What makes someone a good speaker?

3. How much do you talk during school?

4. About what kinds of things do you like to talk?

5. In general, how do you feel about speaking in small groups? In large groups?

6. Whom do you know that is a good speaker? What makes her or him a good speaker?

7. If you knew someone who was having difficulty talking in front of a large group, how would you help him or her?

8. Would you like to be able to perform better when speaking?

Table 4.5   Assessment Purposes

	Speaking	*Listening and Viewing*
Phonological level	To determine fluency in decoding words	To assess phonological awareness
Vocabulary	To practice new speaking vocabulary words with correct pronunciation and usage	To acquire new listening vocabulary words
Oral reading	To practice fluency (speed, accuracy, prosody)	To practice listening for rhythm and sounds of language patterns or visual cues
Presentation: enunciation, stress, wait time	To practice speaking clearly and distinctly, with emphasis on important words	To listen for varying levels of emphasis to determine what is important
Narration	To practice organization and delivery of stories	To listen for meaning and organizational story patterns
Information	To deliver information in a clear, concise, and complete manner, including directions for performing a task	To measure completeness of thought and gather complete and accurate information, including the ability to follow directions to perform a task
Persuasion	To practice convincing others about information or decision making	To critically listen to evaluate information or make a decision
Problem solving	To think out loud; express ideas for reflection and understanding	To evaluate possible solutions and strategies for problem solving
Multiple perspectives	To introduce varying viewpoints and offer peer response to assist in evaluation	To consider various viewpoints and accept peer response for further personal evaluation
Data collection	To collect information through interviews or surveys	To practice listening, collecting, and sorting data
Comprehension strategies	To practice comprehension strategies (e.g., drawing conclusions, cause-effect, compare-contrast, problem-solution)	To practice with literal and inferential comprehension strategies (e.g., drawing conclusions, cause-effect, compare-contrast, problem-solution)
Critical thinking	To question and analyze ideas; to share critical views with others	To question and analyze ideas and authenticity of information
Communication	Communicate to express ideas	Communicate to express ideas
Relationships	To establish and maintain relationships	To establish and maintain relationships
Language arts	To scaffold for other language arts (reading, writing, listening, and viewing) to develop thinking and communication skills	To scaffold for other language arts (reading, writing, and speaking) to develop thinking and communication skills

Phonological instruction and assessment progress from teaching understanding of word, syllable, and phoneme levels to rhyming activities to blend, match, segment, substitute, recognize, and reproduce sounds. Matching first initial sounds, then final sounds, and lastly medial sounds in words provides a progression for assessing student listening skills and understanding. Practice in segmenting spoken words through rhyme, alliteration, manipulation, sorting, and spelling activities is an appropriate way to assess and practice phonological awareness. It generally begins with larger linguistic units (words and syllables, such as *cat*) and proceeds to smaller linguistic units (phonemes to focus on phonological units such as *c-a-t*) and then to increasingly longer words (*catch*).

Assessments may occur in small group instruction but may also be done on a more limited basis by individuals and whole classes when appropriate. Some common phonological awareness instruments usually are included in independent reading inventories and early reading tests. See Figure 4.2 for examples of the types of phonological awareness items often used in assessments.

Assessing Listening Vocabulary

A listening vocabulary consists of the words the student understands upon hearing, and a speaking vocabulary consists of the number of different words the student ordinarily uses for meaningful oral communication. Most children enter school with thousands of words in their listening and speaking vocabularies (Lorge & Chall, 1963). In the earliest grades they learn to identify and decode the printed format of these words. Later, in the upper grades the focus shifts to acquiring additional specialized words and word meanings to match content-area curriculum and more abstract thinking.

Vocabulary assessments have long been recognized for their ability to predict accurate comprehension levels. In fact, comprehension assists in the acquisition of vocabulary as much as vocabulary assists in comprehension. Research has also shown that children who have been read to and have therefore acquired larger listening vocabularies are more proficient in reading achievement tests and language development (Chall, 1987).

Open-ended vocabulary tests may ask students to provide oral definitions or explanations for isolated words. Selected response items can vary from matching lists of definitions and words to selecting synonyms from provided choices. Using cloze tests to strengthen listening vocabularies can be accomplished through the omission of key words from a text that is read or spoken aloud. As words are omitted, students may be asked to insert possible words that maintain accurate continuity in the text, or they may be provided with possible correct choices to complete the text. Some vocabulary assessments provide visual cues and ask students to name objects or actions. See Table 4.6 for examples of items often used on vocabulary tests.

Assessing Listening Comprehension

Listening comprehension levels, as measured by listening to successively more difficult passages in terms of graded readability measures, can help

Figure 4.2   Examples of Items Used in Phonological Awareness Assessments

Many phonological assessments begin with initial consonant sounds, then final consonant sounds, then progress to short vowels, then consonant blends, then long vowel sounds, and finally consonant and vowel digraphs.

Many aural assessments are also accompanied by a picture, as in the following examples.

Raise your hand when you hear a word that starts with the same sound as **can**.

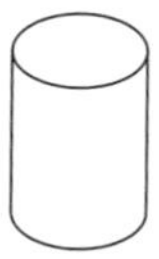

act

cup

trick

cook

circle

Raise your hand when you hear a word that ends with the same sound as **arrow**.

sew

water

few

orange

boat

Raise your hand when you hear a word that has the same middle sound as **pan**.

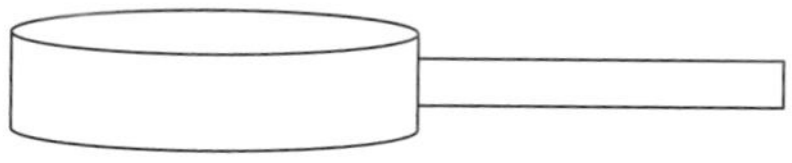

clock

cat

pool

bus

doll

Clap your hands when you hear a word that rhymes with the word **bat**.
  dog, sun, cat, boat, trip, boot, sat, glass

What word is left when you take out the *s* in *spot*?

In **dog** and **fog**, what needs to be changed in the first word to make the second word?
Take away the ___ and add the ___.

Table 4.6   Vocabulary Item Forms Used to Measure Proficiency

Match the words in the first column with the correct meanings in the second column.	
1. Test	a. Fluency in speaking and listening; oral literacy
2. Oracy	b. Judgment of performance as a process or product of change
3. Literacy	c. Ability to read and write, with understanding, a short simple sentence about one's everyday life
4. Assessment	d. Act or process of gathering data in order to better understand the strengths and weaknesses of student learning
5. Evaluation	e. Set of systematic tasks or questions yielding responses that may be quantified so performance can be interpreted

Sort the following words into two or more categories and provide a reason for your group choices.
   frijole, coins, shells, chowder, stamps, linguine, old toys, guacamole

Which word does not belong in the following group? Why?
   bat, alligator, dolphin, grizzly bear, squirrel, elephant
   (Answer: *alligator* is the only reptile)

Using information from the passage you just read, tell which of the following best gives the meaning of the word **stumble**.
   a. fall   b. flip   c. hesitate   d. stagger

Which of the following words means the same as **slow**?
   a.   inert
   b.   gradual
   c.   sublime
   d.   unconscious

Which of the following words means the opposite of **slow**?
   a.   altruistic
   b.   loquacious
   c.   expeditious
   d.   supercilious

A **philanthropist** is most likely to have which of the following?
   a.   loyalty
   b.   tooth decay
   c.   worthwhile causes
   d.   sports equipment

Complete the following sentence to show you know the meaning of the highlighted word.

The **entomologist** seemed worried because _____.

determine a student's independent listening level. Although criteria vary, at least 75% accuracy is suggested as a standard measure of proficiency (Harris & Hodges, 1995). Even before students are old enough to decode texts and read for themselves, they benefit from listening to, responding to, and analyzing text they hear.

The first consideration in assessing listening comprehension is determining the purpose and form for the oral activity and the aspects that will be assessed. Listening comprehension strategies, like reading comprehension strategies, can be explicitly taught and assessed to provide students with the skills necessary for informed literacy learning. Just like proficient readers, good listeners must be actively engaged as they listen. They must have clear goals in mind and be able to evaluate as they listen to determine whether the speaker is meeting their goals. They make predictions as they construct meaning, revise ideas, and question what they are hearing. Good listeners draw from their own background to integrate their knowledge and experiences with what they are hearing. When appropriate, good listeners monitor their comprehension by asking questions about things that do not make sense to them or that are inconsistent with what they already know.

Narration. Listening assessments use different criteria based on the type of text. For example, narrative stories are generally organized around a story line and are told and heard in social contexts. In addition to experiences in listening to and telling stories, songs, and poems of literary value during a language arts block of instruction, children engage in storytelling activities in a variety of informal situations throughout the day by sharing personal experiences with others.

Good listeners are able to visualize the setting, characters, and action in a sequence that provides a logical, easy-to-follow series of events. After listening, they should be able to note main points, recall important details, and summarize the main idea. A quick way to assess students after they have listened to a narrative is to provide them with three statements that they must defend as true or false, based on information presented in the story.

Another means of assessing students' narrative listening skills in both listening and speaking is to use interviews. Older students can practice interviewing skills as part of their listening and speaking assessment activities. First, they interview a classmate about an interesting personal experience as they audio record it. Then, using a graphic organizer, they write it up as a story with a beginning, middle, and end. They share it with the storyteller to ensure accurate retelling. Then they transcribe the recording (or use software that transcribes) and compare the two versions. For a variation, the interviewee could also write a first-person narrative of the same event to compare how close the two versions are. Teams can then write about what they have discovered about some differences in speech and writing. The class can follow up by building a class list of findings.

Information. Assessing listening skills using informational text is somewhat different from using narrative text in that expository text patterns are unlike story grammars commonly used in narratives. Both formal and informal contexts are more common, and formats often include class discussion sessions and school reports. Student listeners often are assessed on their ability to paraphrase, summarize, and recall important details and to determine cause-effect, compare-contrast, and problem-solution relationships.

Assessments in which students practice listening for relevant and irrelevant details may include teacher talk with nonsense information. Students must listen and raise their hands when a sentence delivered in the context of a spoken passage does not make sense to them. For example, "On the way to the lunchroom, stay in a straight line, keep your hands to yourselves, and walk on your heads. Remember, I don't want to hear a sound out of you." This method of listening for incongruity is an important skill that trains students to self-correct in both listening and reading.

Another informal and common assessment teachers use is to stop at midpoint in an explanation and ask students for questions, predicted conclusions, or identification of the purpose or main idea of the talk. This gives students the opportunity to react to what they have heard before listening to additional information.

To encourage reflective listening and practice with note-taking skills, Devine (1982) suggests a practice he calls second-chance listening. After hearing a recorded program or reading, students are asked a series of questions. After responding to the questions, they are given another opportunity to listen to the same information or story. They may correct or add to their initial responses. Devine found that this practice seemed to encourage accurate listening during both activities.

Study guides are also a good means of assessing and assisting students with listening skills. Students can be provided with test questions or statements before listening or viewing. Then, as they listen, they fill in answers and add their own notes. Students can also make up their own questions as they listen. Categories of questions can be provided as a prelistening activity and to activate prior knowledge and understanding of the topic before listening.

Graphic organizers may also help in some listening situations, especially where data collection is part of the listening process. T-charts, Venn diagrams, lists, and matrices can assist in listening for specifically grouped details, as can information frames designed to collect cause-effect, problem-solution, or compare-contrast information.

Testing students' ability to use informational listening skills and dialogue to follow directions is an important part of language arts assessment and can begin in the earliest grades and continue through adulthood. To assess students' ability to follow multistep oral directions, teachers may provide a series of steps for students to follow in actions or in written format, based on their learning levels. For an example of such directions, see Table 4.7.

Students can also be directed to orally repeat information given by a classmate or tell someone who doesn't understand what has been said. Directing students to paraphrase or reexplain a message more clearly than the original speaker are other ways to use experience with informational text to encourage accurate listening and speaking.

Persuasion. Children learn the rewards of persuasive dialogue at an early age. Listen in on any conversation between young siblings with a new toy or

Table 4.7   Listening Assessment Models for Problem Solving

Any number of oral directions can be given to students, who must visually demonstrate their listening comprehension in following directions. The following is a sample of one type of directions we have devised with our students for this activity.

1. At the top left corner of your paper, write your name.
2. In the lower right corner, write the sum of 3 plus 4.
3. In the middle of your paper, draw a circle about the size of a nickel and connect it to your name with a line.
4. If your first name begins with the letter *b, d, j, m, r,* or *t,* draw a connecting line from the circle to the number on the page. Otherwise, draw a line from the circle to the top right corner of the page.
5. If today is a weekend day or if tomorrow is Friday or Saturday, or if yesterday was Sunday or Monday, then put a smiley face in the bottom left corner of your paper. Otherwise, put a W in the middle of the circle.

Following directions. Students work in pairs, with a visual barrier between desks. One has a set of pattern blocks arranged in a design, and the other has an identical set of pattern blocks in disarray. The first student, using only verbal instructions, directs the second student, who cannot see the design, to replicate it within a fixed amount of time. The speaker may or may not view the second student's progress, depending on the desired difficulty level. Students may self-evaluate their roles as listeners and speakers and determine what things might help them improve with the next partner.

between students in the lunchroom when one brings an especially desirable and sharable lunch treat. Their powers of persuasion may amaze you.

Forms and purposes of persuasive texts differ from those of narrative and expository texts in some important ways. Examples of persuasive discourse may include defending an action or proposed solution to a problem, presenting multiple viewpoints on a controversial issue, hosting formal debates on hot topics, participating in panel sessions with varying points of view, listening to and viewing commercial advertisements designed to sell products, and exploring political propaganda to promote reform or change.

Critical listening asks students not just to listen to and comprehend what is heard but to critically analyze the content of what is being said. As listeners, students need to evaluate the speaker's facts, opinions, and possible biases. They need to be familiar with emotive language and propaganda techniques to assess which ones might be in use. As persuasive speakers, students need to practice and evaluate their abilities to express a point of view clearly and succinctly, understand both sides of an argument, determine the effects of word choices and how loaded words carry additional meaning, use questioning to clarify or challenge a different viewpoint, and defend an idea rationally with specific evidence and facts.

Some of the most common persuasive techniques in use for student analysis include the following:

- Bandwagon: Message implies that a desirable group supports the idea or product and plays on fear of being left behind.
- Card-stacking: Message presents only the positive aspects of an idea or product, omitting or discrediting opposing evidence.

- Fear and panic: Message warns or threatens that disaster will result if listeners do not follow a particular course of action or purchase and use a certain product.
- Glittering generalities: Message uses vague, general statements with cherished words or beliefs to encourage approval and acceptance of a product or idea without examining the evidence.
- Name-calling: Message associates negative connotations with a rival idea or product.
- Plain folks: Message attempts to convince audiences that people or ideas are part of the mainstream way of life.
- Testimonial: Well-known and admired celebrities endorse commercial products or ideas without necessarily having the qualifications to make informed judgments.
- Transfer: Message claims that a product or idea is connected to something or someone who is respected to encourage acceptance; sometimes attempts to transfer the prestige of science, medicine, or religion to a product or issue.

Listening and discussion models using various propaganda techniques and emotive language can help students to assess their ability to recognize some of the most common persuasive techniques. See Table 4.8 for survey questions in dealing with critical listening skills.

Oral Presentation Evaluations

Content and Organization. As in writing assessments, assessments dealing with formal oral presentations can use holistic or analytic formats for providing feedback. Many of the same criteria are used in speaking and writing: organization, topic development, syntax and vocabulary, and conventions. Although assessments for speakers include rubrics defining a clear organizational plan, listeners also must assess their ability to determine a speaker's plan of organization. Both speakers and listeners must be able to understand the use of transitional or signal words and distinguish relevant and irrelevant information.

The first few sentences of a talk should engage the listeners and motivate them to continue listening. Often, this is accomplished by connecting with listeners' background information or by showing them why the topic is personally relevant to them. Main points should be delivered and supported in a sequential manner depending on the topic and purpose. Details, examples, facts, and illustrated comparisons should all be related to the main ideas presented. The conclusion should link with the opening and bring a sense of unity and completeness to the talk. For more information on evaluation tools on content and organization, see the rubrics for writing assessments in Chapter 2.

As part of the instructional procedures in oral presentations, students can be guided through an assessment rubric that explains all the elements that will be evaluated. As an extension, students can assist in devising rubrics themselves as they study and practice various aspects of speaking before groups of people. (See Table 4.9 for a set of informal and formal rubrics for primary and intermediate speaking tasks.)

Table 4.8   Critical Thinking Skills Survey

1. Who is the speaker? From what point of view or perspective is he or she speaking?

2. What is his or her purpose in speaking? What is the point of the talk?

3. Is there possible speaker bias? What is his or her motive in speaking to this audience?

4. What is your purpose as a listener?

5. What is the main idea?

6. Which details seem important? Why?

7. Is there a method of organization to the talk? Are transition or signal words or phrases used to indicate shifts in ideas?

8. Can you determine inferences and assumptions the speaker is making and hopes listeners will make as well?

9. Can you recognize examples of facts and opinions and distinguish between the two?

10. In what ways are the support and details given relevant to the topic?

11. What methods or persuasive techniques are being used to convince you?

12. What conclusions do you think the speaker is hoping you will draw?

13. What personal connections have you made with the speaker's message?

14. What questions do you have during and after the talk?

Table 4.9a   Rubric for Primary Oral Presentation

Criteria	Excellent	Okay	Needs Improvement
Stood straight and kept good posture while speaking			
Looked at the audience while speaking			
Gave introduction in first sentences			
Offered good details			
Provided ending to match beginning			
Spoke loudly and clearly so all could hear			
Finished within assigned time limit			
Comments:			

Table 4.9b   Rubric for Informal Oral Presentation

For each item, make a mark at the point on the continuum that best represents the quality of the talk:

Vague purpose or multiple topics	———————— + ————————	Clear purpose; stayed on topic
No identifiable opening or conclusion	———————— + ————————	Effective opening and strong conclusion
Disorganized, hard to follow	———————— + ————————	Logical structure and sequence
Vague, confusing details or explanations; wordy, rambling	———————— + ————————	Clear exposition, appropriate details or explanations, succinct and to the point
Rushed speech	———————— + ————————	Clear, easily understood speech
Monotone voice, volume, and pitch	———————— + ————————	Varied voice tone, volume, and pitch for emphasis
Looked down, never out at audience; facial expression remained the same and no gestures used	———————— + ————————	Made audience eye contact and appropriate facial and expressions gestures
Visual aids difficult to see or understand	———————— + ————————	Good use of visual aids or props (if appropriate)

Make a mark at the point on the continuum that best represents the overall quality of the talk.

("P" or beyond is passing)   ———————— + —P————

Table 4.9c   Rubric for Formal Oral Presentation

	Delivery (worth about 20% of total points)	Articulation, Grammar, Voice Tone (worth about 20% of total points)	Content of Talk (worth about 40% of total points)	Effort (worth about 20% of total points)
Distinguished (or *WOW!*) (91–100)	Comfortable, steady posture. Seems at ease with the audience. Involves many audience members with eye contact and gestures to keep them engaged. Oral performance is enthusiastic, polished, and professional, as well as interesting or even entertaining. Sophisticated.	Vocal expression is enthusiastic and varied to suit purpose and to keep audience engaged. Sentence structure is mixed. Active words are selected deliberately and used effectively. Stayed within specified time limits.	Highly creative. Compelling introduction and conclusion; purpose is abundantly clear early on; conclusion finalizes purpose strongly. Gives listeners deep insight into topic or persuades audience completely of purpose. Transitions essential details and information artfully. Abundant information and evidence to support points.	Evidence of substantial preparation time; student is working at highest potential. There are no errors in content or details. Student chose a challenging topic. Well-thought-out revisions are obvious. Visual aids, when used, are clear and effective and displayed at appropriate times.
Proficient (or *Very Good*) (81–90)	Alert yet relaxed stance. Seems sincere in communicating message. Uses audience eye contact and gestures with some proficiency. Oral performance is professional and interesting. Excellent delivery manner.	Most vocabulary is sophisticated and used properly. Sentences are varied and help listeners maintain interest. Although most words are easily understood, others are beyond the audience's understanding. Pitch, volume, and articulation are appropriate. Stayed within specified time limits.	Solid, catchy introduction; solid conclusion; purpose of review is clear in intro; clear topic sentences. Purpose is clear. Provides vivid picture and deep understanding of topic. Sophisticated transitions. Creative presentation with an appropriate amount of evidence.	Evidence of organization and practice time. Student is working near highest potential. Few errors apparent in content or details. Topic is interesting, and student exhibits interest in it. Visual aids, when used, add to the quality of the presentation.
Satisfactory (or *Fair*) (60–80)	Oral performance is adequate but not compelling. Posture stiff and stilted or too relaxed for the situation.	Spoke clearly and slowly but sometimes too soft or too loud to suit purpose. Uses simple words and takes few	Requirements are barely met. Gives basic account with little or no insight or thought. May be	Adequate amount of time is evident. May exhibit similar errors from previous talks with little or no

	May seem involved at times but seems uninvolved at others. Little eye contact with the audience; if used, gestures seem artificial and unnatural. Moments may be engaging, but overall, work is needed to improve delivery.	risks. Vocabulary may be dull or repetitive. Series of simple sentences or long run-on sentences sometimes make it difficult to understand and tedious for listening. May have finished before or after the specified time limits.	predictable or awkward; not enough evidence from text to support point of view. Transitions are simple or lacking. Basic needs of introduction and conclusion are met, although intent may not be totally clear; clear topic sentences; intro and conclusion meet minimum length requirement. May report facts without insight.	improvement. Although some revisions are apparent, more are needed to achieve proficiency. Visual aids, when used, may not enhance the presentation or may distract from the purpose.
Poor (or Needs Additional Work) (0–59)	Oral performance is inadequate and monotonous. Little effort is made to engage the audience. Aimless pacing or nervous shuffling distracts audience. Eyes shift to ceiling or floor. Nervous gestures; giggles. Much practice with delivery is needed.	Misuses basic vocabulary. Difficult to listen to because of a number of distracting errors. Words are slurred. Voice too soft to be heard at times. May speak too quickly to be understood at times.	Intro or conclusion is either too short, missing, or confusing. Reports facts without insight or opinion. Requirements are met in a simple way. Uses sweeping generalizations with no supporting examples; little or no evidence; missing or confusing transitions; information is unfocused or confusing.	Little evidence of effort or interest in topic. Repeated errors; little or no time or care; sloppy; little or no revision evident. Visual aids, if used, do not complement the talk.

Presentation Style. Speaking for formal situations includes not only the message but also the visual and oral presence of the speaker. Assessment instruments include visual presentation factors such as posture, facial expression, and gestures, and also speaking factors such as articulation, pronunciation, enunciation, tone of voice, and stress. The structure of the content is also assessed and varies with the purpose and type of talk being delivered.

One simple assessment to use in helping students recognize effective speaking techniques is for the teacher to record several versions of the same story that range from monotone to expressive speech. Students are given checklists or rubrics to assess which is the best version for listening and responding. By evaluating a range of performances, they can best self-analyze as they prepare their own talks and as they evaluate their completed speeches.

Language-experience stories, in which teachers write down what children say so the story can be reread, are another way to assess young students' articulation, pronunciation, enunciation, tone of voice, and stress. Echo speaking or reading can also assist in evaluating student performance and offer instructional assistance. Replaying recorded student oral performances can help students evaluate and correct speech patterns.

Young children first develop an understanding of English grammar in infancy and early preschool years by listening, responding, and imitating their primary caregivers (Chomsky, 1972). Later in school, language experiences provide students with opportunities to continue to acquire grammar structures in the context of meaning-making situations.

In informal oral discourse, most grammatical rules are suspended, and speakers generally talk in sentence fragments, reorganize ideas as they talk, and have false starts and stops with hesitations, vocabulary substitutions, and grammatically incorrect sentences. However, for formal oral presentations, students are expected to use accepted norms of speech.

Throughout their educational careers, with instruction and practice, students come to understand different speaking registers depending on formal and informal audiences and situations. For example, whereas academic language encourages more complex sentence structures, home language tends to include shorter words, phrases, and clauses with many incomplete sentences. Ideas tend to be strung together with *and, but,* and *or.* Hesitations with pauses, repetitions, and rephrasing and colloquial terms such as *you know, don't you think?, oh, yes,* and *um* all occur with greater frequency in informal settings. Test criteria for formal and informal speaking experiences vary with the situations in which they occur.

Wait time, that is, the time between a speaker's question and a listener's response, is an important consideration for oral communication. Researchers (Rowe, 1986; Tobin, 1987) have found that with additional wait time, student listeners generally increase the length and correctness of their responses. In addition, with larger groups, they found that with extended pauses allowing listener think time, there was more listener participation. Speakers' questions tended to be more varied and of higher quality as well. Having another person act as wait-time monitor can help speakers check this aspect of their speech and improve the communication process for speakers and listeners. Over time, these pauses will become a natural part of their speaking style.

Some students may be helped in delivering and receiving oral presentation through the use of checklists. After discussing the importance of each criterion, students can review the lists before or immediately after a listening or speaking event. See Table 4.10 for checklists for speakers and listeners.

IMPORTANCE OF A VARIETY OF ASSESSMENT ACTIVITIES AND INSTRUMENTS

Listening, speaking, and viewing assessments should be an ongoing part of all instruction. They should be administered at regular intervals throughout the school year and recorded as a self-assessment measure to raise consciousness about accurate listening and effective speaking.

Guided listening-thinking activities, as described by Templeton (1995), allow beginning readers to enjoy and reflect on stories and information beyond their reading abilities. Their use of important comprehension strategies can be assessed within the safety of a teacher-led discussion that is focused on predictions. After initial predictions about story or text content, they can confirm, reject, or revise their ideas as they progress through the listening experience. As in other group activities, teachers can jot down notes about student skills within a discussion group on prepared index cards or checklists.

Think-aloud activities in which the students or the teacher uses speaking and listening techniques to make literacy skills and strategies explicit to an audience are well-documented comprehension strategies. The teacher may model thinking processes or comprehension strategies while reading aloud or solving a problem and also discuss when it is appropriate to use such strategies. Students may also be directed to think aloud while reading to monitor their comprehension and progress with thoughtful strategic thinking (Duke & Pearson, 2002).

Oral questioning and discussion techniques within groups are used in a variety of situations designed to increase comprehension through listening and speaking activities. Palinscar and Brown (1986, p. 772) describe a reciprocal teaching process in which students and teachers take turns leading discussions through "predicting, question generating, summarizing, and clarifying." Klingner and Vaughn (1999) use groups to preview background knowledge before reading, monitor vocabulary and comprehension during reading, and summarize after reading and to generate questions that might be asked on a test. Raphael (1986) offers question-answer-relationship strategies as a way of framing students' listening or reading of a narrative or informational text. Students not only answer the questions but also determine where best to find the answers. They can find some questions right in the story or in information they hear at the literal level. They must infer answers to some other questions by putting together ideas. Still other questions require a combination of inferential and application-level answers concerning what students may already know, and some students' individual questions may or may not depend on what they hear or read.

Grand conversations (Eeds & Wells, 1989) with literary texts and instructional conversations (Goldenberg, 1992-1993) with informational texts give

Table 4.10a Listener's Self-Checklist

1. Do you look at the speaker during the talk?

2. Are you silent while the speaker is talking?

3. Do you show active listening behaviors; that is, smile, nod, react to what is said?

4. Do you think about what is being said?

5. Can you summarize what the speaker has said in your own words?

6. Can you ask relevant questions to extend the speaker's ideas or message?

7. What are some other topics you might like to hear from this speaker?

Table 4.10b Speaker's Self-Checklist

1. Did pronunciation flow smoothly?

2. Was voice clear and expressive?

3. Did facial expression fit the mood of the talk?

4. Were nonverbal gestures appropriate?

5. If applicable, did the visuals add to the talk?

   • Did visuals seem helpful?

   • Were visuals prepared in a professional manner?

6. Did audience seem attentive and interested?

7. Were there any parts you would improve in your next speech?

students opportunities to discuss what they have read, heard, and think. Using turn-taking protocols, students participate in talking about themes, personal connections, questions, or ideas they have about a text and may build on other students' ideas, or they may ask for additional information from a previous speaker. Procedures allow brief comments by all students so that all have a chance to participate. Teachers may use the checklist provided in Table 4.11 to document students' participation.

Literature circles (Daniels, 2002) and book clubs (Raphael, Pardo, & Highfield, 2002) include literary discussions that are situated in the social context of peer-led book conversations. Within the framework of book-group discussions, literacy and oracy are more than the sum of their language arts elements; that is, reading, writing, speaking, listening, and viewing. It is the interaction with others that reflects students' thinking about, knowing about, and sharing their worlds.

FORMS AND PRODUCTS

Standardized Tests

Most state standards have included listening and speaking skills in their indicators; however, these skills have proved difficult to measure. A number of standardized assessments with reliable normed benchmarks for comparison have been developed over the years. The Educational Testing Service (ETS) has offered the Cooperative Primary Tests for primary grades. In these tests, students listen to words, sentences, stories, poems, or informational texts and then demonstrate their ability to identify information, recall facts or story elements, interpret ideas, and draw inferences, usually by marking appropriate illustrations. The Sequential Tests of Educational Progress: Listening Comprehension (STEPS) assessment, also by ETS, has been in place with alternative forms for older grade levels for almost 50 years. Level 4 is designed for intermediate grades (4 through 6), and Level 3 targets Grades 7 through 9. After listening to passages, students are tested on listening-comprehension tasks such as identifying main ideas, recalling details, sequencing ideas, and defining vocabulary. The tests also include some interpretive items such as determining the significance of details, connotative vocabulary meanings, and relationships between ideas. Evaluative items include critical reasoning such as distinguishing fact from fantasy and relevant from irrelevant details, defending opinions, judging the validity of ideas and reliability of support, evaluating the organization and adequacy of spoken materials, judging the ability of a speaker to achieve his or her purpose, and awareness of rhetorical devices used to influence thinking.

ETS has recently added the new Test of English as a Foreign Language Internet-based test (IBT) in U.S. test centers with a speaking component. The focus of this assessment is to determine how well students read, write, and speak in combination. Test items may ask students to listen to a recording and read a passage, are then speak about both. Their responses are digitally recorded and then downloaded by experts to grade. For additional information on ETS assessments, visit their Web site at http://www.ets.org.

Table 4.11   Teacher Checklist for Individual Oral Participation on Narrative Text

Name	Date	Date	Date	Date	Date	Date
Shared opinion						
Made prediction						
Asked relevant question						
Constructed new meaning						
Summarized or paraphrased (S/P)						
Compared						
Contrasted						
Suggested possible cause and effect						
Provided possible solution to problem						
Appeared to be inattentive by unintentionally repeating another speaker						
Interrupted out of turn						
Did not stay focused; veered off topic						

Classroom-Based Tests

Although many oral language assessments tend to emphasize more formal products rather than the more typical natural discussion processes, both types of speaking and listening are important to consider. Informal records of student progress in listening and speaking may take the form of anecdotal records, written notes or summaries, audio or video recordings, checklists, surveys, rubrics, or evaluation forms. Both student and teacher input are desirable for these records to be meaningful and to assist with student learning.

Some creative classrooms offer a variety of talk-show formats, PowerPoint presentation notes, comic book panels or storyboards, Web sites, and visual displays and exhibits among the artifacts they collect to demonstrate student achievement in oral and visual skills.

FINAL THOUGHTS

Based on research studies that have confirmed the connections between proficiency in oral expression and literacy (Pinnell & Jaggar, 2003), learners must be provided with more opportunities for oral and visual language practice as tools for communicating and learning. "Oral language is the foundation not only of learning and schooling but of our living together as people of the world" (Pinnell & Jaggar, 2003, p. 881). Students of all ages need opportunities to expand their aural and oral vocabularies and syntax variations, to organize their thoughts into speaking exchanges, and to use speaking and listening opportunities to negotiate meaning. Classrooms rich in high-quality listening, viewing, and speaking events can use assessments to monitor student learning and instructional strategies to best meet students' individual and collective needs.

REFERENCES

Bear, D., Invernizzi, M., Templeton, S., & Johnston, F. (2004). *Words their way: Word study for phonics, vocabulary, and spelling* (3rd ed.). Upper Saddle River, NJ: Prentice Hall.

Buck, G. (2001). *Assessing listening.* New York: Cambridge University Press.

Cazden, C. B. (1988). *Classroom discourse: The language of teaching and learning.* Portsmouth, NH: Heinemann.

Chall, J. (1987). Two vocabularies for reading: Recognition and meaning. In M. G. McKeown & M. E. Curtis (Eds.), *The nature of vocabulary acquisition* (pp. 7–18). Hillsdale, NJ: Erlbaum.

Chomsky, N. (1972). *Language and mind.* New York: Harcourt Brace.

Clay, M. M. (1998). *By different paths to common outcomes.* York, ME: Stenhouse.

Daniels, H. (2002). *Literature circles: Voice and choice in book clubs and reading groups.* Portland, ME: Stenhouse.

Devine, T. G. (1982). *Listening skills schoolwide: Activities and programs.* Urbana, IL: National Council of Teachers of English.

Duke, N. K., & Pearson, P. D. (2002). Effective practices for developing reading comprehension. In A. E. Farstrup & S. J. Samuels (Eds.), *What research has to say about reading instruction* (3rd ed., pp. 205–242). Newark, DE: International Reading Association.

Eeds, M., & Wells, D. (1989). Grand conversations. An exploration of meaning construction in literature study groups. *Research in the Teaching of English, 23*(1), 4–29.

Ehri, L., Nunes, S., Willows, D., Schuster, B., Yaghoub-Zadeh, Z., & Shanahan, T. (2001). Phonemic awareness instruction helps children learn to read: Evidence from the National Reading Panel's meta-analysis. *Reading Research Quarterly, 36*(3), 250–287.

Goldenberg, C. (1992–1993). Instructional conversations: Promoting comprehension though discussion. *The Reading Teacher, 46*(4), 316–326.

Harris, T. H., & Hodges, R. E. (Eds.). (1995). *The literacy dictionary: The vocabulary of reading and writing.* Newark, DE: International Reading Association.

Heath, S. B. (1983). *Ways with words.* New York: Cambridge University Press.

International Listening Association (ILA). (1996). International Listening Association Web site. Retrieved May 31, 2006, from http://www.listen.org/Templates/welcome.htm

International Reading Association and National Council of Teachers of English. (1996). *Standards for the English language arts.* Urbana, IL and Newark, DE: Authors.

Klingner, J. K., & Vaughn, S. (1999). Promoting reading comprehension, content learning, and English acquisition through Collaborative Strategic Reading (CSR). *The Reading Teacher, 52*(7), 738–747.

Leavitt, J. (1847). *Easy lessons in reading; for the use of the younger classes in common schools* (3rd ed.). Watertown, NY: Knowlton & Rice. (Original work published 1823)

Lorge, I., & Chall, J. S. (1963). Estimating the size of vocabularies of children and adults: An analysis of methodological issues. *Journal of Experimental Education, 32*(2), 147–157.

Marzano, R. J., & Arredondo, D. E. (1986). *Tactics for thinking.* Aurora, CO: Mid-continent Regional Educational Laboratory.

Moffett, J., & Wagner, B. J. (1992). *Student-centered language arts, K–12* (4th ed.). Portsmouth, NH: Boynton Cook/Heinemann.

Palinscar, A. S., & Brown, A. L. (1986). Interactive teaching to promote independent learning from text. *The Reading Teacher, 39*(8), 771–783.

Parker, F. W. (1896). *Talks on teaching.* New York: E. L. Kellogg. (Original work published 1883)

Pinnell, G. S., & Jaggar, A. M. (2003). Oral language: Speaking and listening in elementary classrooms. In J. Flood, D. Lapp, J. R. Squire, & J. M. Jensen (Eds.), *Handbook of research on teaching the English language arts* (2nd ed., pp. 881–913). Mahwah, NJ: Erlbaum.

Raphael, T. E. (1986). Teaching question-answer-relationships, revisited. *The Reading Teacher, 39*(6), 516–522.

Raphael, T. E., Pardo, L. S., & Highfield, K. (2002). *Book club: A literature-based curriculum.* Lawrence, MA: Small Planet Communications.

Rowe, M. B. (1986). Wait time: Slowing down may be a way of speeding up. *Journal of Teacher Education, 37*(1), 43–50.

Smagorinsky, P., & Fly, P. K. (1994). A new perspective on why small groups do and don't work. *English Journal, 83*(3), 54–58.

Sticht, T. G., & James, J. H. (1984). Listening and reading. In P. D. Pearson (Ed.), *Handbook of reading research* (pp. 293–317). New York: Longman.

Templeton, S. (1995). *Children's literacy: Contexts for meaningful learning.* Boston: Houghton Mifflin.

Tobin, K. G. (1987). The role of wait time on higher level cognitive learning. *Review of Educational Research, 57*(1), 69–95.

5

Assessment Portfolios

"This year, I am going to use portfolios with my students," said Mary. "This summer I learned about them at a class, and I think they will help me know more about my students' reading and writing."

"I have heard about them, too, but aren't they hard to do and don't they take a lot of time? I don't think my students would know why they were selecting work to go into one. How would I ever get them to make good selections, and how would this help them to grow as students anyway?" replied Sandra.

"I don't think it is going to be easy at first. I just worry that my students don't see all the assessment we do as very important," Mary said. "I want them to know about themselves as readers and writers, and I think portfolios might help. Do you want to try with me, Sandra? Maybe we could team up and share our successes and difficulties."

"I'm not sure; let me think about what this might mean for a bit. Maybe we can talk more later," Sandra said.

This discussion was shared between two third-grade teachers as they planned for their new academic year. Mary was enthusiastic about bringing portfolios into her classroom. She believed that portfolios would help her know her students betters as readers and writers, and she thought they would help her students see the purpose of assessment. Sandra, her colleague, was not convinced that her students were ready to make thoughtful decisions about what should be included, and she was not sure that portfolios would be beneficial to her or her students. Many teachers share similar concerns in that they see strengths and difficulties with implementing portfolios in their classrooms.

Portfolios became prominent in classrooms in the 1970s and 1980s as a complement to process writing. Students began to collect their work in portfolios to document their writing throughout a year or as they worked through a project. In some schools, portfolios were established as an essential part of the school's assessment plan, and each year a student's portfolio was embellished with a new year's worth of accomplishments in writing (Hebert, 2001; Tierney & Clark, 1998). In some schools and classrooms, teachers moved beyond a singular focus on writing and expanded portfolios to include other parts of the curriculum such as spelling, reading, math, science, and social studies.

Making the concept of portfolios a bit more complex, Valencia (1998) described five types of portfolios, each with a different purpose.

- Showcase portfolios highlight the best work of students. These might be used to share with parents at an open house, for example.

- Documentation portfolios keep a record of performance and achievement and are used by teachers to inform instruction.

- Evaluation portfolios typically are completed by teachers and report classroom-based achievement to others.

- Process portfolios describe the process of a learning activity. For example, they might document the process of completing a report in which all drafts are shared to show changes from draft to draft.

- Finally, Valencia described a composite portfolio in which any of these elements might be included. The composite portfolio is targeted to a broad audience of teacher, student, parent, and principal.

For this chapter, we are using a combination of these types of portfolios to create an *assessment portfolio*. The assessment portfolio might include the following:

- Formal assessment data
- Informal classroom-based assessment data
- Student samples (some may document the process as well as the product)
- Student, parent, and teacher self-reflections with accompanying documentation

For this assessment portfolio, we are envisioning that teachers, students, and parents may all contribute. The goal of this portfolio is to document student growth over time. It fills in the details that appear in the results of more formal assessment. For instance, all third graders are expected to take a criterion-referenced test. This test shows how well students are doing in meeting grade-level expectancies in reading, writing, and other subjects as determined by the district or state at a single time. Although these data are important in determining the success of students in meeting curriculum expectations, they do not show the growth students make from the beginning to the end of the year. That is the goal of an assessment portfolio. It tells the story behind such numerical data as standard scores, percentiles, and even Annual Yearly Progress (AYP) standing. It provides direction to teachers for ongoing instruction.

WHAT IS AN ASSESSMENT PORTFOLIO?

Assessment portfolios are collections of student work that represent a student's performance in the everyday activities of the classroom. Samples generally are collected at specified times of the year so that a student's growth can be documented systematically. The samples are selected carefully so that they represent the quality of student work rather than a huge, unwieldy collection. Teachers may also design specific informal assessment activities to be included. Many of these were described in Chapters 2, 3, and 4. Students and teachers collaborate on what is selected and included for evidence in the portfolio. There may also be a section where the teacher keeps informal and perhaps formal assessment data (Frey & Hiebert, 2003). And finally, there may be a section where parents and students contribute artifacts that support literacy growth at home.

Portfolio Organizational Structures

Teachers often structure each student's portfolio with specific sections so that each section contributes to a more thorough knowledge of the literacy strengths and needs of students. Importantly, there is no one best structure. Teachers may start with one organizational structure and find that they are missing important assessment data and that they need to revise and include new sections or delete current ones. Each section results in different artifacts and various people (teacher, student, parent) contributing. The following are a few possible configurations of an assessment portfolio.

Portfolio Organization Around Literacy Elements

Section 1: Informal assessment centered on phonological awareness and phonics, comprehension, fluency, vocabulary, and writing (selected by teacher)

Section 2: Student work documenting each literacy element (selected by teacher and student)

Section 3: Additional documentation of each element (e.g., artifacts from home, books read throughout the year, writing samples throughout the year) (selected by teacher, student, and parent)

Portfolio Organization Around Formal and Informal Assessments

Section 1: Formal assessment (collected by teacher)

Section 2: Informal assessment (collected by teacher)

Section 3: Student work guided by teacher, usually accompanied by a rubric (collected by teacher and student)

Section 4: Additional documentation (selected by teacher, student, and parent)

Portfolio Organization Around Informal Assessment, Product, and Process

Section 1: Informal assessment (collected by teacher)

Section 2: Student work documenting literacy knowledge (collected by teacher and student)
   a. Documentation centered on each literacy element
   b. Specific focus for each collection time (e.g., fluency, comprehension, vocabulary)
   c. Evidence of ability to write to traits or different genres

Section 3: Student work documenting literacy process (collected by teacher and student)
   a. Evidence of writing a story, report, poem, etc., going through the revision and editing process
   b. Evidence of deepening understanding throughout the reading of a novel or informational text
   c. Evidence of process to increase fluency
   d. Evidence of process to develop vocabulary

Section 4: Additional documentation (teacher, parent, and student)

Teachers have also organized portfolios to match district or school curricular goals. They begin by listing the learner outcomes expected in a quarter or semester. Then, once these outcomes are detailed, they brainstorm with students about what evidence might support each outcome. Table 5.1 shows a guide sheet for this portfolio organization.

Finally, teachers may organize portfolios so that students' current accomplishments, areas they are working on, and future goals become the structure. When using this structure, students are expected to document their current accomplishments and areas they are still working on. Goals can be mutually determined with a teacher, and ways to achieve the goals are also recorded. Table 5.2 shares an example of this structure, and Table 5.3 provides a blank copy for teacher use.

All of these structures facilitate learning about students over time and target instruction. They support conversations about students and their learning and offer tangible ways to ground these discussions. And they provide opportunities for students and teachers to reflect on literacy learning and to set goals for future learning.

Portfolio Reflections

As work is selected for the portfolio, a reflection synthesis is included for each entry. The reflection piece is important to portfolios because it supports metacognitive thinking about learning. This thinking allows students to become engaged in their own learning processes and to set personal goals for continued learning. It supports a collegial relationship between teachers and students as they work together to facilitate learning (Danielson & Abrutyn, 1997). The portfolio reflections also make learning more concrete to students

Table 5.1   Learner Outcome Guide

Portfolio Organized Around Targeted Learner Outcomes	
Learner Outcomes	*Supporting Evidence*
Communicate effectively in writing	Journal entries
	Reader response log
	Letter to parents about report card
	Research report on mammals
	Pen pal letter
Comprehend informational text	Response entries
	Quick writes
	Venn diagram about mammals and reptiles
	Research report on mammals
Use strategies to comprehend text	Self-report while reading, documented in log
	Informal Reading Inventory
	Peer and teacher observation

Table 5.2   Accomplishments, Current Learning, and Goal Structure for Portfolio

Name	Things I Can Do	Things I Am Working On	Goals
Reading comprehension	I can read chapter books. Evidence: Log of books Accelerated Reader quizzes Reading response logs	I am working on reading informational text. Evidence: Science textbook Book on whales Report	I want to be better at understanding what I read in informational books. What I will do: Look at important words and find out what they mean. Use notes as I read. Make a chart.
Reading fluency	I can read books at the fourth-grade level. Evidence: The level on the book My fluency chart	I am working on reading about 100 words a minute at the fifth-grade level. Evidence: Fluency chart	I want to be able to read about 120 words in a minute at the fifth-grade level. What I will do: Choose text and practice. Keep a fluency chart.
Vocabulary	I can read longer words. Evidence: Vocabulary notes in my reader response journal Word sort of *-able* and *-ible* words	I am working on understanding the words in my social studies book. Evidence: I looked them up and wrote definitions. I found them in the book and tried to figure them out.	I want to learn about words in my math book. What I will do: I will make a list of them. I will see whether any of them are alike. I will see whether I can figure out what they mean with my dictionary.

Table 5.3 Blank Copy of the Accomplishments, Current Learning, and Goal Structure for Portfolio

Name	Things I Can Do	Things I Am Working On	Goals
Phonics and decoding			
Comprehension			
Fluency			
Vocabulary			
Writing			

in that they can see their strengths and learning needs as they explore a piece of work or the results of an informal assessment. Teachers can synthesize what is most important about the informal assessment, for example. A teacher might document that Michael is fluent with narrative text but is struggling when he reads informational text, and she can show Michael how this determination was made. This observation provides information that guides the teacher's instruction in that she will provide additional scaffolding to support Michael's reading of informational text, and it heightens Michael's attention when he is reading informational text.

Students also indicate why they selected a piece of work. For students as well as parents and teachers, a developmental process is evident in the syntheses supporting a piece of evidence. In Table 5.4 there are several examples of reflective entries from Jeremy, a fifth grader. When scanning his entries it is easy to determine that his first reflective entries were global: "I picked this because list of books, becauses it shows I know how to read." Later his entries are more specific and demonstrate that he is aware of the nuances of his developing literacy abilities.

The sophistication of Jeremy's reflections grew as his teacher nudged him to be more specific about his learning. Teachers can often become discouraged when students initially say, "I picked this piece because I liked it" or "I picked this piece because I worked on this story." Through thoughtful conversations with students about their work, teachers can extend these naïve reflections to more purposeful ones that highlight the complexities involved in learning. For example, a teacher might say, "I find this part of your story very interesting. I think I know what your characters are feeling. Can you tell me what you were thinking as you wrote this part?"

Portfolios without reflections are merely a collection of student work and assessments. They lack the reflection that fosters a critical evaluation of current learning to guide future goal setting. We believe that the reflections,

Table 5.4   Jeremy's Reflection Entries

September

I picked this list of books because it shows I know how to read.

December

I picked this chart because it shows how I can read more fluently. I was slow at first, and I stumbled over words. Now I can read informational text at fifth-grade level with accuracy at about 100 words a minute.

April

This word study page from my notebook shows that I understand the root *mis*. It took me a while to figure it out. I had to find many words and then determine what *mis* meant. Now when I read I am not confused about the meaning of words with *mis* in them.

June

This report shows how I found information from many places. Then I figured out how to share all of the information. In my first draft, you can see that it doesn't always make sense. In later revision, I organized better. I think this piece shows how I focused on organizing information.

though time intensive, are the critical aspect of portfolios that move them beyond a showcase of student work.

WHAT ARE THE ISSUES SURROUNDING PORTFOLIOS?

Getting Started

The best way to get started is to keep the purpose of the assessment portfolio in mind: showing student growth and learning over time. Given this purpose, it becomes obvious that not all the work a student completes will be included in the portfolio. The following schedule facilitates work with portfolios:

July-August:	Choose the organization of the portfolio. Prepare portfolios for students. Determine a place in the classroom to store portfolios and a place where work that might enter a portfolio can be stored. This might be a large envelope or an accordion folder, for instance.
September:	Introduce the portfolio process to students. Establish the routines for portfolios. Have students write an initial entry for the portfolio such as goals for this year or who they are as a reader or writer. Share the portfolio process with parents.
September:	Include informal assessments in portfolios. Write a reflection of what was learned through this assessment (strengths and needs of student).
October:	Meet with students (and parents) individually to share what was learned through assessments. Have students select work for the portfolio and write reflective notes. Add information shared by parents about home literacy events and products.
November:	Have students work with a partner or in small group to add to their portfolios. Meet with partners or groups of students to discuss portfolio entries.
December:	Synthesize the portfolio to document growth for the first half of the year. Establish learning goals for next half of the year. Meet with parents and students to share the portfolio or add to it.
January:	Revisit portfolio goals. Add additional informal assessment and share with students.
February-April:	Continue to add to the portfolio and to discuss with teacher, student, partner, or groups of students.
May:	Final assessments, entries, and formal assessment data. Students reflect on end-of-year accomplishments. They

reflectively write about learning. Teachers complete all assessments and reflectively write about student learning.

June: Students and teacher synthesize the portfolio to document growth for the year. Share with parents and students.

Summer: Revise portfolio process if needed.

Teachers might also determine that in each month a particular part of the portfolio will be considered. So for one month only reading might be addressed, the next month writing, and so on. This narrowed focus often is chosen as teachers and students become comfortable with the portfolio process. Importantly, there is no one best way to facilitate work with portfolios. Planning and thinking through the details on how the portfolio process will be implemented are the critical pieces for successful implementation.

Finding Time

Teachers who are trying portfolios for the first time often find that they are time intensive. They notice that they need extensive time to become familiar with the process and to structure it. Moreover, students are slow at determining what they want to include in their portfolio and reflective comments. Certainly, teachers are right about the additional time it takes to successfully bring portfolios into a classroom (Valencia, 1998).

Initially, teachers need time to ponder how they might organize their portfolios. This preliminary preparation will streamline the portfolio process once it has begun. Teachers need to consider such pragmatic concerns as where portfolios will be stored and how students will access them. The following are other questions that are important to ponder: Will folders, boxes, file cabinets, or notebooks be used? Will sections be given to students, or will they work through this organization with students? Will all work be kept for a period of time and then students will sift through it to make selections for their portfolio, or will the teacher predetermine which pieces of work will be selected? How often will students add work to their portfolios? Will the whole class be involved during this process, or will the teacher work with small groups of students or individual students? Clearly, teachers need to consider many questions before initiating the portfolio process. We believe that these questions and resulting decisions are best made in collaboration with other teachers who will also bring assessment portfolios to their classroom. Through these dialogues, teachers can share successes, difficulties, and plans for revisions.

Because of the time commitment, teachers must be convinced that there is value to this process. Certainly, the most important reason is that it improves student learning (Polakowski, 1993; Tierney, Carter, & Desai, 1991). Students become more engaged and reflective in their learning. The conversations with individual students guide further instruction and make both the teacher and student responsible for learning. Second, the process becomes more efficient as teachers and students become more familiar with the process. Once students understand the process, they are more proficient at selecting work and identifying why it was chosen. Third, entries can be selected during an independent work time rather than a special portfolio time. Teachers learn to embed the portfolio process into their teaching routines.

As teachers begin with assessment portfolios, it is important to keep the end view in mind. Although the process is cumbersome in August, by November it should be more efficient. Teachers should find that selecting work is more automatic, reflections are more specific, and conversations about portfolio entries are more targeted to future student learning. And by the second year of implementation, teachers might discover that they would be unable to determine student growth without the use of portfolios.

Making the Effort

Certainly, bringing portfolios into a classroom places additional demands on teachers. Using portfolios entails planning and conferring with students, parents, other teachers, and the principal. Through assessment portfolios, teachers realize the importance of differentiated instruction to meet the needs of students. Subsequently, teachers are presumed to have sufficient knowledge of the curriculum and students so that they can target instruction to student needs.

Moreover, assessment portfolios do not replace informal and formal assessments. Rather, informal and formal assessments become a part of the portfolio. Formal and informal assessments balance the ongoing collection of student artifacts and reflections that document student growth. Students, parents, teachers, and principals get a rich picture of an individual student's development and his or her achievement in reaching benchmarks on more formalized assessment. Portfolios offer two lenses to view students' learning: a close view of individual student learning and a comparative view of students in a class or grade level. Both views offer information for instruction and for the acceleration of student learning.

Looking Into Assessment Portfolios

Although we have spent time talking about portfolios, often the best way to understand them is to take a look inside. In this section, we share pieces of student portfolios so that teachers can consider what might be important for them to include as they ponder bringing portfolios to their classroom or revising the portfolio process currently in place. The samples are taken from primary and intermediate students' portfolios.

Teacher Entries

This section focuses mainly on informal assessment data that teachers may include. We have selected examples from Michael's fifth-grade portfolio that show growth throughout an academic year. His teacher began each year by having students independently complete Informal Reading Inventory (IRI) assessments. When they were finished with this assessment, she completed a summary sheet. When looking at Michael's summary sheet, she noted that he was independent on material through a ninth-grade level. Michael could certainly have continued with the IRI levels, but his teacher thought that knowing that he was so far beyond grade level was sufficient for instructional purposes. This information supported her decision to place Michael in a small reading group with a similar student; they read together, and she joined them for book discussions. She did not believe it was necessary for Michael to participate in grade-level reading events because he was so far beyond grade level. Table 5.5 shares the record his teacher created, and Table 5.6 shows his responses to one of the passages he read during the IRI.

In addition to the IRIs, Michael's teacher had all of her students participate in a spelling inventory. She used these data to determine how students represented words so that she would know exactly how to target phonics instruction, structural word study (e.g., how to add prefixes or suffixes to words), and vocabulary instruction (see Bear, Invernizzi, Templeton, & Johnston, 2000, for details). Table 5.7 shows the results of Michael's spelling inventory at the beginning of fifth grade. Michael demonstrates sophisticated knowledge about words. He is struggling with the less common words such as *caught* (*cot*), *inspection* (*inspecne*), and *puncture* (*punkshere*). This result lets his teacher know that for Michael the best word instruction will be vocabulary because he has mastered phonics and structural word knowledge.

When his teacher shared these informal assessments with Michael and his mother, she first read her reflection to them. Table 5.8 displays her reflection.

Michael's teacher periodically added informal assessments to her students' portfolios throughout the year. She chose to do this at the beginning, middle, and end of the year. She collected similar informal assessments at each point in time for easy comparisons. In the examples that follow, end-of-year assessments for Michael are shared. When they are placed side by side, it is easier to see Michael's academic growth in reading and spelling.

Michael's teacher did not require him to retake the IRI in narrative text; rather, she moved him to informational text. She wanted to make sure that Michael was fluent and comprehended both narrative and informational text. Table 5.9 displays the summary of his results and also one passage that he responded to. Michael's informational text reading is slightly below the level of his narrative reading. This result matched Michael's preference for text during independent reading. He preferred to read fantasy rather than informational books. His final spelling inventory showed growth, although it is subtle. Michael was able to represent more of the least common words, but he still struggles with *-tion* and *-ture* (see Table 5.10).

Many teachers complement informal assessments with formal assessments. For example, fourth-grade teachers often include the end-of-third-grade criterion-referenced test results as part of their beginning-of-the-year assessment entry. In conjunction with a student entry, they include the results for all third-grade students in their school so they have an idea of how this student compares with other students. For example, Heidee scored a 30 for reading, demonstrating that she mastered 75% of the curriculum. When compared with other students at her school, Heidee did quite well. The average score was 21, with 52% of the reading curriculum mastered.

Other test data that might be considered are national achievement test results or state writing assessment results. Figure 5.1 and Table 5.11 share these results. The difficulty with results such as these is that the test or writing

Table 5.5   Summary of Michael's Informal Reading Inventory Results

Name <u>Michael</u>   Date <u>September 20, 2004</u>

Results: Independent _____9+_____ Instructional _____ Frustration _____

Level 1

   0–1 questions missed = Independent   Continue? Yes _____ No _____
   2   questions missed = Instructional
   3+ questions missed = Frustration

Level 2

   0–1 questions missed = Independent   Continue? Yes _____ No _____
   2   questions missed = Instructional
   3+ questions missed = Frustration

Level 3

   0–1 questions missed = Independent   Continue? Yes _____ No _____
   2   questions missed = Instructional
   3+ questions missed = Frustration

Level 4

   0–1 questions missed = Independent   Continue? Yes _____ No _____
   2   questions missed = Instructional
   3+ questions missed = Frustration

Level 5

   0–1 questions missed = Independent √   Continue? Yes ___√___ No _____
   2   questions missed = Instructional
   3+ questions missed = Frustration

Level 6

   0–1 questions missed = Independent √   Continue? Yes ___√___ No _____
   2   questions missed = Instructional
   3+ questions missed = Frustration

Level 7

   0–1 questions missed = Independent √   Continue? Yes___√___ No _____
   2   questions missed = Instructional
   3+ questions missed = Frustration

Level 8

   0–1 questions missed = Independent √   Continue? Yes ___√___ No _____
   2   questions missed = Instructional
   3+ questions missed = Frustration

Level 9

   0–1 questions missed = Independent √   Continue? Yes___√___ No _____
   2   questions missed = Instructional
   3+ questions missed = Frustration

Table 5.6   Michael's Informal Reading Inventory Responses

Name <u>Michael</u>   Date <u>September 15, 2004</u>

Level 9

1. Where and what time of day was this story set?

    It was set in the night of Cresent City.

2. What was the problem facing the writer of this story while he walked up Rampart?

    A man was following him.

3. How did the policeman react to this story?

    The policeman just thought he was joking.

4. What happened after he left the policeman?

    Some men gathered around him and made him go into the building.

5. How did the writer of this story solve the problem?

    He grabbed the man and asked what he was doing.

6. Who was Nero, and how would you describe him?

    He looked evil and he was like a gangster.

7. What series of events got the person in this story into such trouble?

    The weird man and the group of men that circled him.

8. What did the author do after he was released?

    He never told anything about it and he never went back.

Table 5.7   Michael's Spelling Inventory

Name <u>Michael</u>	Date <u>September 10, 2004</u>
1. bed	11. preparing
2. ship	12. popping
3. drive	13. cattle
4. bump	14. Cot (caught)
5. when	15. Inspecne (inspection)
6. train	16. Punkshere (puncture)
7. closet	17. cellar
8. chase	18. Pleaser (pleasure)
9. float	19. squirrel
10. beaches	20. Fourtnneite (fortunate)

sample is not present, just the results. Therefore, teachers, parents, and students can see the results of the assessments; however, they do not have the actual questions or writing to return to. Based on a classroom's results or a school's results, a determination might be made to teach vocabulary more systematically. For individual students, there are rarely direct connections between these assessments and instruction.

Table 5.8 Michael's Teacher's Reflection

Fall, Fifth Grade: Michael

Reading: Michael is reading narrative text beyond the expectations of fifth grade. He is fluent and accurate as he reads. Beyond the information from the Informal Reading Inventory, I noticed that he considers other students' points of views when they discuss what they are reading. He also knows to slow down when the reading gets harder. When he writes about his reading, he relies on summaries. I want him to move into deeper explorations of text.

Spelling: Michael is proficient with phonics and structural word knowledge. He needs to expand vocabulary knowledge—root instruction.

Writing: Michael is not as thrilled about writing as he is about reading. He seems frustrated when his attempts do not match the quality of his reading. We need to work together to help Michael grow as a writer.

Schools, grade levels, and individual teachers decide which assessments to include in this portion of a student's portfolio. Teachers may decide to include similar informal assessments throughout the year to show student growth. Teachers could also vary the informal assessments to demonstrate an area that is currently being studied. For example, at the beginning of the year, a teacher may be most focused on comprehension. Toward the middle of the year, this focus may have shifted to fluency, and therefore the items included are representative of growing accomplishments in fluency. Later in the year, the shift might be to vocabulary, and again the collected documentation would reflect this focus. The important part of this portfolio is to document student growth in a way that best supports classroom instruction.

Figure 5.1 Results From a Norm-Referenced Test

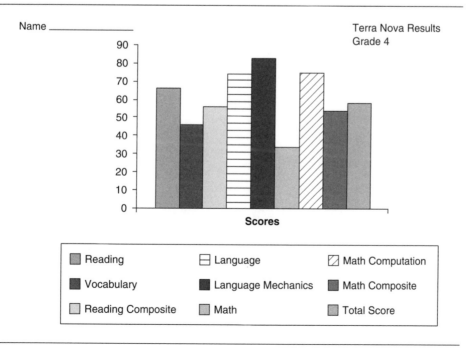

Table 5.9   Michael's Informal Reading Inventory Summary and Passage Results, End of Year

---

Name <u>Michael</u>   Date <u>May 2005</u>

Results: Independent 8   Instructional 9   Frustration Above 9 (Informational Text)

Level 7

     0–1 questions missed = Independent √   Continue? Yes <u> √ </u>   No <u>   </u>
     2 questions missed = Instructional
     3+ questions missed = Frustration

Level 8

     0–1 questions missed = Independent √   Continue? Yes <u> √ </u>   No <u>   </u>
     2 questions missed = Instructional
     3+ questions missed = Frustration

Level 9

     0–1 questions missed = Independent √   Continue? Yes <u>   </u>   No <u> √ </u>
     2 questions missed = Instructional
     3+ questions missed = Frustration

Level 9 Questions and Answers

1. What two reasons were given for visual illusions?

    They are caused by ideas in the brain. (only 1 idea)

2. What is an example of a lateral inhibition illusion?

    A bull's eye

3. The Gateway Arch is an example of what distortion?

    Lateral

    (length distortion)

4. Explain how length distortion occurs.

    Our eyes work better side to side then up and down.

5. What's an example of Hermann's Grid?

    A high office building

6. How does Hermann's Grid affect what you see?

    It makes eyes see gray spots at the corner of squares.

7. Explain why the old axiom "Don't believe everything you see" is true.

    They said the bridge is just as long as it is tall, so when we think it is longer than taller that is wrong.

8. How does the tendency of eyes to move more easily from side to side rather than up and down affect the way we perceive tall objects?

    They look higher than they are.

Table 5.10   Michael's Spelling Inventory, End of the Year

Name Michael	Date May 2005
1. bed	11. preparing
2. ship	12. popping
3. drive	13. cattle
4. bump	14. caught
5. when	15. Inspecsion (inspection)
6. train	16. Punctuere (puncture)
7. closet	17. cellar
8. chase	18. Pleasuere (pleasure)
9. float	19. squirrel
10. beaches	20. Fortinite (fortunate)

Table 5.11   Results From a State Writing Assessment

State Proficiency Examination Report

Name Mary   School _____   Test Date _____

ID# _____   District _____   Grade _____

Purpose of Writing Assessment

This assessment is part of the State Proficiency Examination Program administered in Grade 4. Its purpose is to provide administrators, teachers, parents, and students with information about student proficiency in writing.

How the Assessment Is Scored

A sample of writing is scored by trained teachers. Each piece of writing is scored by two teachers who independently assign a score of 1 to 5 for each trait. The scores are averaged so each student receives one score for each trait. A score of 3 indicates that the writer has demonstrated adequate achievement of his or her grade level in that trait.

Mary's scores are as follows:

Ideas 3.5   Organization 4.0   Voice 3.5   Conventions 4.5

Student Entries

This section targets entries that students thought were important to include to document their growth as literacy learners. There is greater variation in students' selections, and each portfolio is unique to its owner. We have included portfolio entries that identify a student and his or her strengths and needs as a reader and highlight a student's academic goals for a year, with samples of reading, word study, and writing that students have included for a variety of reasons.

The first two examples were included by students so that readers of their portfolios would know about them as readers and writers. For instance, in Table 5.12, Josie wrote how she became a reader in fifth grade. After Josie included her entry, she wrote, "I chose this entry because it lets everyone know that I am a good reader. I like to read many books at one time and that is why I check so many out at the library."

Table 5.12 Josie's Writing About Being a Reader

Me as a Reader

When I was in the. . . . Oh yah the first grade, I hated to read because I didn't know how. But one day when we were at the library I decided to go I checked out a book and I read it. It was so interesting that I read the whole book. That's how I started to read. Now I love to read because when we go to the library I check six or more out. When I read it feels like I'm there. It's really fun to read that's why I get so excited when I read. So that's me as a reader.

Mark decided to present his goals for his sixth-grade year as a way to begin his portfolio. He wrote,

My first goal is to do better in math. I think I need to multiply faster. My next goal is to read informational books better. I have a hard time remembering what I read in them. My next goal is to try to do my best on all of my assignments. Sometimes I get sloppy just to get done. So when you look through my portfolio you should see that I met my goals this year.

In this statement Mark identified several goals that were personally meaningful. He was also astute in providing evidence that he had accomplished each of them. Through his documentation, anyone could see that he had met his goals.

The next examples represent students' documentation of reading, word knowledge, or writing. Unlike their teachers' more systematic entries, these are broad based and targeted to students' goals for learning. In Table 5.13, Laquisha described a tutoring plan to show that she has developed as a reader and can plan a tutoring experience for a younger student.

Another entry by Laquisha demonstrated that she was an accomplished writer. She included her brainstorm, her first draft, a revising and editing checklist that was completed by another student working with Laquisha, and her final draft. In Table 5.14, pieces of each of these parts are included.

Table 5.13 Laquisha's Tutoring Plan

Tutoring Plan for Nathan

Book: *Pancakes for Supper*

Questions

Before reading: What do you think the book is about? Have you heard of it before?
During reading: Do you think she likes it when her sister calls her Lilly Lolly Little Legs? Would you like it if somebody called you a name?
After reading: Did you like the ending? Do you think you can read this book yourself now?

Activity: Write about how to make pancakes. Maybe draw a picture.

Reflection

I picked this plan because it shows I can read this book and turn it into a lesson for Nathan. I picked it for him because he likes pancakes. It showed that I think questions before, during, and after reading are important.

Table 5.14   Laquisha's Writing Accomplishments

Brainstorm

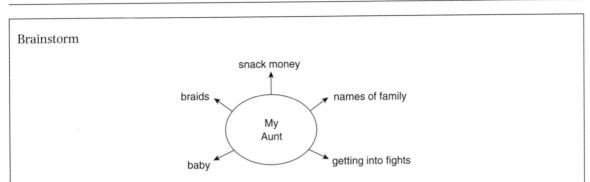

First Draft

This is about my aunt. She's nice and she has three kids. She loves flors. She has a baby but the babie is mean. He kicks an fights and pinches and it hurts. Her kids have big bird. She has a lot of snacks. After we do homework we get to go outside.

Peer Revision and Editing Guide

	Good	Okay	Revise
Organization			
Has a good, attention-getting opening	√		
Tells things in the best order			√
Has a good ending		√	
Details add to main idea		√	
Sentences			
Sentences are complete		√	
Sentences begin differently	√		
Word Choice			
Words are vivid		√	
Words don't repeat	√		
Mechanics			
Punctuation		√	
Spelling		√	

Beginning of Final Draft

This story is all about my aunt. She is nice and she has three kids. She loves flowers. She has a baby but the baby is mean. He kicks and fights and pinches and it hurts.

I stay at my aunt's house. Every time when we get out of schools, my Aunt Betty gives us a snack. Once we finish our homework we can go outside and play with our friends.

Reflection

I chose these parts to my story so I could show what I do when I write a story. First I think about what to write. Then I get my ideas down. I like to meet with Ellen because she gives me good ideas to make my writing better. Then I work on it and get it into a final draft. When I write the final draft the computer helps me find spelling mistakes. Before I just used to write a first draft and then I was done.

Laquisha has built a powerful case for her development as a writer. Her beginning of her final draft shows how she has reorganized her ideas and presented them in a more coherent way. She has fixed many convention errors as well.

The next student example was included by Taylor as support for her ongoing word knowledge. She said she chose this sample because "It is my best work. It shows that I know how to add *y* or *ly* to words. I never make mistakes now." Her sample is shown in Table 5.15.

Table 5.15 Taylor's Word Study

happily	sunny
slowly	rainy
nicely	funny
poorly	sloppily
silly	honestly

The last example is from Nathan's reading response notebook. He explained, "I picked this because it shows that when I read I think of what happened and then what happened. I am thinking while I read. I would never get into the trouble that Ramona does." Figure 5.2 shows one piece of Nathan's entry that demonstrates his comprehension of longer text.

The student entries shared here represent a wide range of choices to document reading and writing. Teachers can open up this documentation process to students, or they may constrain it so that certain pieces of work are required to be inserted. There is no best way. Often teachers who are new at portfolios require students to include specific entries. As teachers become more comfortable with the portfolio process, they hand over more of this responsibility to students because they know that students will most often select the most personally meaningful examples of their reading and writing development.

Parent Entries

Parents have included entries to document their children's literacy activities away from school. The following are several entries that support literacy learning outside school. In first grade, Mrs. Lane asked parents to write to her about their children. She used these letters as ways to better understand each student and to learn about their home literacy experiences. One parent wrote to her about her son, Jaryd,

> My son, Jaryd, is a kind boy. He never wants to get into trouble. We will help him with his homework. We know that you will teach him to read. Sometimes Jaryd reads with his older sister. We have little time to read with him.

This letter was the beginning of ongoing conversations between Mrs. Lane and Jaryd's parents. She knew that if she wanted Jaryd to read at home, it would have to be easy for him unless she could get his older sister to help. She also

Figure 5.2   Nathan's Comprehension Entry

knew that Jaryd's parents wanted him to do well in school, and they had taught him to follow the teacher's directions. She used this partnership to support Jaryd in his in-school literacy activities.

The second example comes from Bonnie's parents. Bonnie's teacher asked each parent to write a history of the literacy learning of his or her child. The following is part of Bonnie's literacy history, as written by her mother:

> I read to Bonnie before she was born. I read to her older brother each
> day and then I read to the two of them. If we read a book about a picnic,

then we had a picnic. We did many of the things we read about. We took books with us everywhere we went. If we had to wait in line, I read to her. I think she started to read at about 5. I am not sure though. She never liked to write. It was hard to get her to make any letters. I wrote notes and then read them but she still didn't want to write.

Bonnie's teacher realized that Bonnie was living in a home that valued reading and writing. From her youngest days, she was surrounded by books and saw them as enjoyable.

The final example is from Maria's parents (Table 5.16). When they came to school for a parent conference, they brought a sheet on which they recorded all of the reading that Maria did at home. Maria's father told the teacher, "I brought this because Maria has read all the books we have. Now we go to the library to get her more books." This sample showed Maria's teacher that Maria read daily at home and that her parents were partners in helping her become a reader.

Each of these examples highlights the connections between home and school in supporting children in learning to read. By having parents include portfolio entries, teachers and schools get a richer picture of students' achievement.

Collaborative Entries

This section highlights entries that were included through ongoing conversations between students and their teachers. Importantly, as these entries were selected, teachers conversed with students, and they collaboratively contributed to the reflection entries.

The first entry is Eric's letter to his teacher about his grades. She wanted students to think about why they may have received a certain grade and, if their grade fell below their expectations, what they might do to improve. She kept these letters and asked students to document their progress each quarter. In this way, students came to better understand how their teacher arrived at report-card grades. Table 5.17

Table 5.16 Maria's Reading Record

Books	Date
Gorilla	August 15
Apes	August 30
Monkeys	September 2
Polar Bears	September 14
Harold and the Purple Crayon	September 20
Brown Bear	October 1
Henny Penny	October 9
Teeny Tiny Woman	October 15
Dr. Seuss ABC	October 19

Table 5.17 Eric's Letter About His Report-Card Grades

Dear Mrs. Purcell,

I feel great about my grades because I did pretty good this time. I think I am okay with my A in reading. I think I do good in reading because I am a quiet person and I like to read a lot. I would like to improve my B grade in writing. I think I can do that by thinking about my reports more and working on adding details. The grade I am worried about is my C in math. Math is hard for me. I think maybe I need to work harder at power math. To tell you the truth I don't really like math that much. So it is hard for me.

Your student,
Eric

---

shows Eric's letter. During the quarter Eric and his teacher worked on adding details to his reports and comments about math and his attitude toward it.

The second entry was chosen by Josie's teacher and Josie. Josie had complained to her teacher in her journal, "Vocabulary is tricky. I don't know what all the words mean and then I don't understand." Her teacher responded to this by having Josie collect difficult vocabulary. During the day they found time to chat about confusing words. In Table 5.18 are some of the words Josie found confusing. Her teacher wanted this example included because it demonstrated Josie's need to find meaning in text and a strategy she used to help.

The final entry was chosen by Sandra and her teacher. She completed an interest inventory about reading, and they decided this showed why she chose the books she did during independent reading. She wrote,

> I like chapter books especially ones that have a lot of them, like Junie B. Jones. Once I start reading one then I want to read them all. I pick books that my friends tell me about. I think those are the best.

This piece of the inventory told Sandra's teacher that she felt proficient reading series books, especially those recommended by her friends. From this bit of information, her teacher queried her students and made sure that she had copies of the books most preferred by her students.

Table 5.18 Josie's Confusing Vocabulary Words

From *True Confessions of Charlotte Doyle*

Balustrade
Abomination
Impulsively
Tolerant

Reflection
  I think this shows I have improved my vocabulary. At first I just looked up the words but I still wasn't sure what they meant. Now we talk and look them up and I remember.

Collaborative entries often are determined through a conversation about efforts to learn to read or write more effectively. Through conversation, these perhaps missed efforts become visible and become important documentation of a student's efforts to become literate.

FINAL THOUGHTS

Readers of this chapter surely have noticed our bias toward including portfolios in classrooms. We believe that portfolios offer students, parents, and teachers opportunities for collaboration centered on student learning. Moreover, we believe that assessment portfolios fill the gaps of achievement test results. Portfolios provide a window into the complex literacy learning of individual students over time. By exploring these profiles, teachers can tailor their instruction to be the most beneficial to students. Teachers can also make comparisons across portfolios so that they better understand the learning strengths and needs of all students in their classrooms. Although bringing portfolios to a classroom can be challenging, we believe the results are worthwhile in the learning trajectories of students and the professional development of teachers.

REFERENCES

Bear, D., Invernizzi, M., Templeton, S., & Johnston, F. (2000). *Words their way: Word study for phonics, vocabulary, and spelling instruction.* Englewood Cliffs, NJ: Prentice Hall.

Danielson, C., & Abrutyn, L. (1997). *An introduction to using portfolios in the classroom.* Alexandria, VA: Association for Supervision and Curriculum Development.

Frey, N., & Hiebert, E. (2003). Teacher-based assessment of literacy learning. In J. Flood, D. Lapp, J. Squire, & J. Jensen (Eds.), *Handbook of research on teaching the English language arts* (2nd ed., pp. 608–618). Mahwah, NJ: Erlbaum.

Hebert, E. (2001). *The power of portfolios: What children can teach us about learning and assessment.* San Francisco: Jossey-Bass.

Polakowski, C. (1993). Literacy portfolios in the early childhood classroom. In M. Dalheim (Ed.), *Student portfolios* (pp. 50–55). Washington, DC: Bookshelf.

Tierney, R., Carter, M., & Desai, L. (1991). *Portfolio assessment in the reading–writing classroom.* Norwood, MA: Christopher-Gordon.

Tierney, R., & Clark, C., with Fenner, L., Herter, R., Simpson, C., & Wiser, B. (1998). Portfolios: Assumptions, tensions, and possibilities. *Reading Research Quarterly, 33,* 474–486.

Valencia, S. (1998). *Literacy portfolios in action.* Orlando, FL: Harcourt Brace.

6

Putting Assessment in Perspective

A lady from the principal's office came to the first grade. She had a big pile of papers with little boxes all over them. She smiled at the first grade. "We have some tests for you," she said. "Oh, good," said Anna Maria. "Now we can find out how smart we are" (Cohen, 1980).

This experience is common in elementary schools. Someone, often the principal, appears at the classroom door, and children are cued that it is time to take an important test. In many schools, testing and other forms of assessment and the information that is secured through them become the focus for school and grade-level meetings. Often, varied assessment results are pieced together so that teachers and principals can determine grade-level and school trends from the data results. For instance, teachers may place the informal assessments they conducted in their classroom next to the more formal assessments students participated in. Through this process they better understand the purposes of each assessment and their intended audiences; most important, they note any changes that are necessary in their literacy instruction or curriculum in their classrooms, grade levels, and schools.

This chapter takes a broad look at assessment in an elementary school and the assessment data that are collected within a school and beyond its boundaries. In particular, assessments are explored for their potential influence on states, districts, schools, teachers, parents, and students. We begin this exploration by considering international evaluation studies, then move to assessment studies in the United States. From this expansive focus on assessment we narrow to districts, schools, classrooms, and finally to students. Although we believe the goal of all assessment is to improve student learning, some of the following assessments are not necessarily explicitly linked to student instruction or learning. They are used to rank all U.S. students or to rank states. Although this information is important to consider, it rarely is directly connected to in-school instructional practices.

OVERVIEW OF ASSESSMENT DATA

International Assessment Data

Two international studies are important for teachers to be aware of. The first is the Trends in International Mathematics and Science Study (TIMSS). Since 1995, 45 countries have participated in a study of trends in math and science achievement that assesses fourth and eighth graders. In 2003, U.S. fourth and eighth graders exceeded the international averages in both math and science. More detailed information on the results of this long-term study is available at http://nces.ed.gov.

More specific to the content of this book is the Progress in International Reading Literacy Study (PIRLS). PIRLS studies trends in literacy achievement for fourth graders from 50 countries. It was first conducted in 2001, and they are conducting another assessment in 2006. In 2001, U.S. fourth graders were ranked fourth in narrative reading comprehension and thirteenth in expository comprehension. Overall, U.S. fourth graders ranked ninth. These results indicate that it would be important for schools to consider the differences in narrative and expository comprehension and to determine ways to facilitate stronger achievement in expository text. For further information about this study, see http://www.pirls.org.

The information gleaned from international studies provides a context for exploration of U.S. trends. It also targets, in general, suggestions for curricular change. This was evident in the brief exploration of the PIRLS results in achievement. The results demonstrate uneven comprehension achievement in narrative and expository or informational text. Schools could be expected to devote more instruction to the teaching of expository text so that students perform equally well with both types of text. This instruction probably would begin in kindergarten and continue throughout elementary school so that students can refine their knowledge and comprehension of expository or informational text.

National Assessment Data

The National Assessment of Educational Progress (NAEP) is considered the nation's report card (see http://nces.ed.gov). Over the past 35 years, NAEP has provided an independent measure of what students across the United States know and can do in reading, mathematics, science, writing, and other core subject areas. NAEP has been reporting state-by-state results since 1990. NAEP selects a sample large enough to ensure valid and reliable results but generally does not include every student in the grades being assessed. For example, in 2003 about 190,000 fourth-grade students in 7,500 schools and about 153,000 eighth-grade students in 6,100 schools participated in the reading assessment. Schools located in states or districts that receive Title I funds are that receive Title I funds are required to participate in biennial NAEP reading and mathematics assessments at Grades 4 and 8 if they are selected. School participation in all other assessments is voluntary. Children chosen to participate represent hundreds or thousands of students in their state and the nation.

Some of the general results reported in 2004 were as follows:

Reading scores of students at ages 9 and 13 are higher than in 1971.

The percentage of 9-year-olds reaching level 150 (discrete reading tasks) and level 200 (partially developed skill and understanding) was higher in 2004 than in 1971 or 1999.

The percentage of 13-year-olds reaching level 300, understanding complicated information, was higher in 2004 than in 1971.

Girls outperformed boys at all ages in reading.

Black students' average reading scores were higher in 2004 than in 1971.

Hispanic students' average reading scores were higher in 2004 than in 1975.

In 2005, NAEP reported data on 10 large urban schools districts. The average reading scores in fourth grade for the districts were lower than the national average, except for Charlotte, North Carolina, which was higher, and Austin, Texas, which was the same. Similar results were reported for eighth graders, with most districts scoring below the national average except for Charlotte and Austin, which were the same. The NAEP Web site, mentioned earlier, presents more fine-grained analysis of these results.

NAEP uses specialized reading performance-level descriptions that are unique to this assessment. These descriptors are important because NAEP expects sophisticated performance from students, and often the performance-level title implies that students did not do particularly well when in fact their performance was satisfactory. The following are the descriptions for the five levels of performance.

- Level 350: Learn From Specialized Reading Materials
  - Readers can extend and restructure the ideas presented in specialized and complex texts. Readers can understand the links between ideas even when they are not explicitly stated and can form generalizations. Success at this level indicates the ability to synthesize and learn from specialized reading materials (scientific text, essays, historical documents).

- Level 300: Understand Complicated Information
  - Readers can understand complicated literary and informational passages about topics they study in school. They can analyze and integrate less familiar material and provide reactions and explanations to the text. They can find, understand, summarize, and explain relatively complicated information.

- Level 250: Interrelate Ideas and Make Generalizations
  - Readers use intermediate skills and strategies to search for, locate, and organize the information they read in relatively lengthy passages. They can make inferences and reach generalizations about main ideas and the author's purpose. They can search for specific information, interrelate ideas, and make generalizations.

- Level 200: Demonstrate Partially Developed Skills and Understanding
  - Readers can locate and identify facts from simple informational paragraphs, stories, and news articles. They can understand specific or sequentially related information.

- Level 150: Carry Out Simple, Discrete Reading Tasks
  - Readers can follow brief written directions. They can select words, phrases, or sentences to describe a picture or interpret simple written clues to identify an object. They can carry out simple, discrete reading tasks.

Like those of international studies, NAEP results present a descriptive picture of the state of reading achievement in the United States. States, districts, and schools can use these data to understand general trends in reading achievement in the United States, and they can explore the results for their particular state. For example, the most current results show improvement in reading achievement for fourth and eighth graders. Schools might consider the expectations of NAEP and in particular the reading performance-level descriptions and scrutinize their reading curricula to see whether these expectations are revealed and whether there are opportunities for students to practice these skills and strategies.

State Assessment Data

States also assess students to determine the state's overall proficiency in certain subject areas. Districts and schools can use these assessments to identify how their students measure up in comparison to all students in the state. By visiting the Web site for the Council of Chief State School Officers at http://www.ccsso.org, educators can learn about the assessments required in each state. For example, in Alabama students in third and eighth grade take the Stanford Achievement Test in math and reading. They also take the Alabama Reading and Math Test. Children in kindergarten through second grade participate in the Dynamic Indicators of Basic Early Literacy Skills (DIBELS) assessment. In states such as New Jersey and Nevada, students participate in state-developed criterion-referenced tests. Oklahoma and other states use a combination of state criterion-referenced tests and nationally standardized norm-referenced tests such as the Stanford 9.

All states administer some type of standard assessment at targeted grade levels (Orlofsky & Olson, 2001). These assessments are useful because they can be administered easily to large numbers of students and are scored consistently, thus ensuring reliability of the results for comparative purposes.

Often these tests result in lists of schools that are exemplary, high achieving, adequate, or in need of improvement. Moreover, schools are labeled as meeting the expectations of the No Child Left Behind Act or not. Each state has identified the criteria for Annual Yearly Progress (AYP), and once a year the determination is made as to whether schools have achieved this benchmark. In each state the benchmark is a moving target in that every 2 years or at some other interval the expectations increase to achieve benchmark status. For example, in one year 30% of students in third grade are expected to read at grade level for that school to achieve AYP, and in the next 2 years this percentage might increase to 39%, making the benchmark more difficult to achieve. Additionally, there are expectations that all children regardless of race or family income, for instance, will attain this benchmark. Details about specific states can be found at http://www.ed.gov.

In addition to state assessments such as the criterion-referenced test or standardized normed tests, states typically assess students in writing in the fourth or fifth grade and in eighth grade. States have developed prompts and rubrics for this assessment. The rubrics usually are organized around traits such as ideas, organization, voice, and conventions, although states often use different names for the assessed trait or may include others. Typically, groups of teachers within the state are trained to score the writing samples. As with other assessments, each student receives scores for each trait that determine whether he or she has achieved the benchmark. For example, Josie received the following scores: Ideas, 3.5; Organization, 4.0; Voice, 3.5; and Conventions, 4.5. Because 3 is the benchmark score, Josie is considered to be a proficient writer. Scores are then aggregated to determine the overall success of schools within a state. Table 6.1 shows a profile of writing scores for a school compared with district and state results. The results for this school are not particularly positive in that the school has more students who have not achieved benchmark than in the district and the state and fewer students who have reached benchmark than in the district and state. Consequently, the school knows that student writing is not where it should be as measured by this assessment, although there is no indication of what instruction would best facilitate students' development and more proficient achievement. Teachers at this school will need to meet and brainstorm about how they might specifically target instructional changes to improve student writing.

Like international and national data, state data provide information to schools that show strengths or needs for the overall curriculum. Schools can use these data as a focus for school improvement, knowing that ongoing

Table 6.1   School, District, and State Writing Score Sample Report

1 Developing			2 Approaching			3 Meeting			4 Exceeding		
School	District	State	School	District	State	School	District	State	School	District	State
24.7%	18.4%	22.4%	47.2%	22.2%	24.1%	25.8%	33.3%	33.2%	2.2%	26.1%	20.4%

student data will facilitate the selection of specific instructional content and strategies to increase and deepen student learning.

District Assessment Data

School districts often require additional assessments in their schools. For instance, they may also have criterion-referenced tests tied to their grade-level standards in reading, math, social studies, and science. Or they may expect students to engage in norm-referenced tests at grade levels not required by the state.

Many schools participate in federal or state grant activities that also require assessments. For instance, schools with Reading First funds have norm-referenced tests required for first, second, and third graders as outcome measures. They also participate in ongoing assessments, called progress monitoring, to determine student growth.

Similar to Reading First expectations, many districts have recently designed progress monitoring assessments in reading and math. Students are expected to participate in these assessments three or four times per year. The goal is to determine whether students are making adequate progress at fixed intervals throughout the year. If students are not successful, schools can respond with tutoring or interventions for struggling readers.

Progress monitoring assessments can take a variety of forms. They may be tied to district standards, elements of literacy (phonological awareness, phonics, fluency, comprehension, and vocabulary), or a core reading program. The goal of these assessments is to support students who need additional instruction and to determine how students in a school are doing in relation to reading benchmarks.

District assessments, similar to state assessments, allows the superintendent and school board to determine how well individual schools are doing. They can also document similar areas of success or difficulty for students in a specific discipline or grade level. These assessment results are also used as a comparison for state results. Districts might see that students are more successful on district criterion-referenced assessments than on the state assessments. They then need to decide whether this result is appropriate or whether alignment is needed in the district assessments so the results are more similar. District assessments also provide an opportunity for the district to assess curricular elements that are unique to the district.

School Assessment Data

Not surprisingly, schools also engage in assessment practices. In some schools, teachers are expected to perform certain informal assessments in literacy, for example, and then grade-level teachers discuss the progress of students. We observed that at Monroe Elementary School, teachers in fourth grade had students write to various prompts during the year. After each assessment, teachers collected the samples and evaluated them based on a rubric. Then teachers stapled each paper on a bulletin board by student proficiency. Teachers evaluated the overall writing proficiency of their students. They looked for positive trends in student writing, and they also considered writing issues centered on struggling students. These discussions resulted in changes in the curriculum and in some cases small group work to support students in areas of difficulty.

In addition to informal assessment, teachers in some schools have students complete unit or theme tests that are part of their core reading series. In this way, schools can determine which students are proficient in the just-taught skills and strategies. They can evaluate their students' achievement to determine whether they are reaching grade-level expectations. And they can determine which students need intervention or tutoring to meet these expectations. Schools can use these data in planning for instructional support and in acquiring additional materials, if necessary, to meet students' learning needs.

For schools that have literacy coaches, this school-based assessment can help them target classrooms and students for instruction. For example, if a teacher usually has students who struggle with vocabulary assessments from the core program, the literacy coach can work with the teacher to enrich vocabulary instruction in this classroom.

Classroom Assessment Data

These data are at the heart of instruction in a classroom. They have a central position in all assessment discussions (Hiebert & Calfee, 1992). Classroom-based data are the closest to actual learning; therefore, they are most likely to influence instructional decisions. They are also ongoing in that as teachers teach, they often informally assess what students learn and how they learn it. They are often so intertwined with teaching that it is not possible to separate assessment from teaching.

Many chapters in this book provide examples of literacy assessments that teachers might conduct. It is important that classroom-based literacy assessments occur routinely so that teachers can document student growth. Most of the previously listed assessments in this chapter occur once and provide only a static picture of student achievement. Classroom assessment is different because it includes multiple kinds of assessment that provide a rich, more complex understanding of a student's strengths and needs in literacy over time.

Eight significant principles are connected to classroom-based literacy assessment (Cooper, 1997):

1. Assessment must be an ongoing process. It is not a single test but rather multiple assessments that occur throughout a school year.

2. Assessment is an integral part of instruction. Assessment is an ongoing part of instruction. It allows a teacher to determine how a student is doing and to compare students within a class. It provides an opportunity for teachers to revise instructional plans.

3. Assessment is best when it is authentic. Teachers get the best information about student reading and writing when students engage in reading and writing activities that are grounded in instruction.

4. Assessment is a collaborative, reflective process. When students collaborate with other students or the teacher, they reflect on what they have learned and how they can improve. Through this process, teachers and students share the responsibility for learning and evaluation.

5. Assessment is best when it is multidimensional. Teachers learn more about students when they have students engage in a variety of assessment tasks. For example, teachers and students learn more about their literacy achievement by evaluating their writing, retellings, and responses to their reading than through any one of these samples alone.

6. Assessment should be developmentally and culturally appropriate. Assessment tasks that have single right answers limit the ability of students to demonstrate partially constructed knowledge. Similarly, children from different cultures may respond differently to various assessments. Teachers need to be mindful that certain assessments may limit students' responses.

7. Assessment is expected to identify student strengths. Children learn best when they move from what they know to new strategies or skills. Teachers need to identify student strengths, not just areas or skills that need to be developed.

8. Assessments must be developed around the current scientific base of how students learn to read and write. Teachers need to revisit assessments to determine whether they are current and reflect today's understandings of the essential elements of literacy.

Importantly, classroom assessment data are linked to classroom instruction. Teachers use these data to group students and to determine the most effective instruction to help students achieve.

USES OF ASSESSMENT

The overall picture of assessment sometimes is overwhelming to teachers. They begin to believe that all they do is prepare students for assessments, give the assessments, and then prepare for the next assessment. However, we believe that teachers must understand the audiences and purposes of assessment. And we agree with teachers that sometimes there are too many assessments that are redundant and consume precious teaching time.

One way to consider assessments is how often they are given. The assessments that are given once per year or once in a student's elementary school career are generally used for comparison purposes to determine how well a nation, state, district, or school is performing. They are furthest from students in that only aggregated data are considered. These are the assessments that often find their way to newspaper headlines and televised news reports. We find out how well or how poorly U.S. students are doing in comparison to students in other nations. We find out whether U.S. students can read more proficiently than they did in past years. We find that a school that was once considered adequate in student performance is now on a watch list, and the school is given support to raise these achievement data. These assessments serve accountability purposes.

The first problem with such assessments is that they are only a brief sample of what students know. Many districts and schools become frustrated because they are often known only by the results of these high-stakes assessments rather than the learning and teaching that occur daily. Second, teachers find that precious class time is spent in preparing students for these assessments. Linn (2000) cautioned that students who practice only the format of a test are less likely to learn the content. Therefore, they do not demonstrate enhanced achievement on the assessment. Moreover, Valencia (2002) reported that if students are prepped for one reading test and then take a different test, their scores often drop because they have not learned how to transfer their reading skills to a new situation. A third concern is that if teachers narrow their curriculum to what is tested, important student learning experiences are eliminated. Finally, these assessments provide overall scores, often after students have moved up in grade level. The lack of timely feedback makes it unlikely that teachers or students can use the results for future learning.

In contrast to one-time assessments are the ongoing, classroom-based literacy assessments that are directly tied to students and to instruction. Unlike one-time assessments, these rarely appear in newspapers or on news reports because they are not used for accountability. However, they drive instruction and student success. These data allow teachers to make moment-to-moment decisions about students. These assessments are collaboratively reviewed with parents, students, and teachers so that all parties are involved in improving student outcomes. Table 6.2 compares one-time and ongoing literacy assessments.

Another way to consider assessment is through the purposes and audiences for assessment. As seen in the previous descriptions of assessment, not all assessment is targeted to students and classroom practice. Standardized norm-referenced tests are used for comparison purposes, and the audience is typically policymakers, superintendents, principals, parents, and the general public. Criterion-referenced tests are also used for comparison purposes, but because the content of these assessments reflects the curriculum, the audience is broader and includes policymakers, superintendents, principals, parents, and teachers. School-based and classroom-based assessments typically are internal to the school and are used to construct appropriate instruction or to provide interventions. The audiences for these assessments are students, teachers, parents, and principals (see Table 6.2).

Table 6.3 highlights various assessment measures. Some are grounded in classroom practice and are tied to instruction. Others are high-stakes assessments in that they stand alone and may connect to instruction but are not an integral part of it. Others might be used to describe the process of learning and others the products resulting from learning. Taken together they form a full portfolio of potential assessment practices. Although many possible assessments are presented in this table, and more could be identified, we are not implying that teachers should use them all with students. Teachers need to

Table 6.2   Continuum of Assessments

One-Time Literacy Assessments (criterion-referenced tests or standardized norm-referenced tests)	Ongoing Classroom-Based Literacy Assessments
Distant from students, looking at group data	Close to students, looking at individual student data
Overall evaluation or comparison purposes	Classroom instruction purposes
Audience: policymakers, superintendents, teachers, principals, and parents	Audience: students, teachers, parents, and principals

Table 6.3   Portfolio of Literacy Assessments

Assessing Processes	Assessing Products
Anecdotal records	Oral or written responses
Interviews	Literature response logs
Conversations	Reflection logs
Response groups for writing	Portfolios
Book club discussions	Narrative and informational writing
Retellings	Journals
Participation in lessons	Projects
Running records	Notebooks
Oral presentations	Responses through visual arts
Drafts, revisions	Reports
Note taking	Presentations
Problem-solving written entries	
Learning centers	
Assessment Tied to Instruction	*High-Stakes Assessment*
Inventories	Standardized normed tests
Checklists	Criterion-referenced tests
Informal Reading Inventories	School, district, and state tests
Interest and attitude surveys	Writing tests
Unit or theme tests	
Informal literacy assessments	
Diagnostic tests	

target the informal classroom assessments to the needs of their students. In most cases the high-stakes measures are mandated, and teachers are not free to decide whether students will participate in them.

We believe that putting all of the many assessments into context helps teachers tease out the functions of each type of assessment. Importantly, although standardized normed tests attract the most public attention, classroom-based literacy assessments have the most power in changing student learning because they support and guide student achievement.

A FEW FINAL ASSESSMENT CAVEATS

In this section we describe a few issues centered on assessment practices that we have observed in schools. Sometimes they highlight the need to consider a more student-centered view of assessment, and other times they highlight the need to ensure that the assessment product and evaluation tool match.

Moving From a Static Picture to Growth

Often, in the frenzy around assessments targeted to accountability, schools lose sight of student growth. They become most interested in the results of a single assessment. We are not discounting the importance of one-time accountability assessments; we are emphasizing the importance of considering student growth over time.

In some schools, this view of assessment occurs only in single classrooms, where teachers informally assess students at the beginning of the year and then periodically throughout the year. They document the growth of students in comprehension or vocabulary, for instance. They are able to articulate to parents and principals the specific growth model for each student in the classroom.

At other schools, teachers within and across grade levels monitor the growth of students. For example, as students move from one grade to another, teachers confer about students and their particular literacy strengths and needs. Future teachers have a growth picture of the students entering their classrooms that helps them target instruction.

Principals and teachers in such schools routinely consider their literacy curricula and determine what changes are needed to support student growth. In some cases, it might just mean tweaking their curriculum. In other cases, it might mean providing additional support for certain students, such as struggling readers or students learning English as a new language. Once these changes are implemented, principals and teachers study the results by considering student learning.

Importantly, schools that take a long-term look at student growth through multiple assessments enact important changes in curricula that enhance their students' learning. They are mindful of accountability assessments, but they choose to focus on the day-to-day learning of students because they know this learning will be recognized in improved student growth, as measured on large-scale accountability assessments.

Using Assessment Data for Individual Student Instruction

As mentioned in the previous section, schools look to their data to support instructional decisions. For instance, if through progress monitoring assessment they find that several first-grade students are not making progress in phonics, they immediately arrange their instructional day so that these students receive additional instruction. They might have an instructional aide meet with these students daily to provide additional systematic instruction in phonics.

In some schools, they may find a time each day when all first-grade teachers, for instance, work with targeted groups of students. The students walk to their respective teacher and receive additional instruction targeted to their strengths and needs (a walk-to-read model). This model makes use of all grade-level teachers and sometimes instructional aides as well. Each teacher or aide is responsible for instructing a small group of students. During this additional half hour or 45 minutes, teachers target instruction specifically to student needs. For example, they may highlight vocabulary for students learning English so that they comprehend the story they will soon read. Another teacher may support grade-level readers in more thoroughly understanding a piece of informational text. Importantly, teachers know that these students must be reassessed continually so that when their needs change, they can move to an appropriate group.

Most of the previous discussion was centered on struggling readers or students learning English, but teachers also use these groupings to enhance and deepen the knowledge of accelerated students. In this way, these students are given opportunities to meet their capabilities, and they are not limited to learning just grade-level concepts and skills. We have seen students compare characters across stories to understand how their characteristics played out in the various plots, for example.

Making Sure That the Assessment Is Scored With the Correct Rubric

Throughout this book, we have offered numerous assessment rubrics and checklists. We believe that they will help teachers and schools assess their students in ways that support instruction and further learning. However, we have seen situations in which teachers mistakenly used the wrong assessment rubric to evaluate student work. Not surprisingly, the evaluation underrepresented the knowledge and skills of a student. The following is one example to ponder.

Kennady, a third grader, was asked to write during a writing workshop. Her teacher supported students' writing to their own topic and provided time for students to revise and edit their work. Kennady took advantage of this time and wrote an informational text about fairies. Her text is shared in Figure 6.1. She chose fairies as her topic, but she did not write a story.

Her teacher met with her for a conference and had her change some of her sentence structures and word choices. What she did not do was help Kennady transform her writing to a narrative. This change was important because

Figure 6.1   Kennady's Fairy Writing

A World of Fairies

Do you love fairies? Ya, I love fairies! Sometimes I think of them as twinkling stars, and sometimes they are very mischievious when they tie girls' hair to their head boards a night.

Elves are different kinds of fairies which can be as tall as a fourth grader. Sprites can be as small as your pinky toe.

Did you know that summer blue fairies are drama queens? They are like little actors! Do you want to hear an imitation? Ok, here it goes "What!? I can't go to Fairytopia Hills Mall with my friend! This is the end of my life!" do you get the picture?

Now do you love fairies?

Flower fairies are the most playful. They like to turn lily pads into boats and race them in little ponds. (They also like to weave daisy chains.) All of the flower fairies are named after flowers like daffodils, daises, and the rose. They love to collect due every summer morning.

I like the Green-Eyed Elf the best because it is the only girl elf in the fairy kingdom. And Brownies... well, I think brownies are the bomb! They are so cool! They can use their minds to tie a string with out even touching it!

Kennady's teacher evaluated her writing as a narrative, and her writing did not meet this expectation. As a result, this piece of writing was scored as not meeting benchmark, which was correct. It did not, for it was not a narrative, and it was scored for not having a beginning, middle, and end with a plot in evidence.

Kennady's teacher is laudable for her instruction in many ways. She provides time for students to write daily, she allows them their choice of topic, she has them revise and edit, and she has created rubrics to score writing so students and parents can see growth, strengths, and areas for improvement. However, she has limited herself to one universal rubric, assuming that her students will write only narratives. When this didn't happen, she still scored student writing as if it were a narrative and told students that their writing was not up to standard when they did not write a narrative.

We wondered how this scenario would have played out if one of the following had occurred:

- Grade-level teachers met and considered student writing. They evaluated each other's students so they could determine consistency in their scoring. They noted students who showed growth and those they worried about so that they could target and enhance their instruction through conversations with peers.

- The teacher gave the rubric to students before writing so that students knew what kind of writing they were expected to create.

- The teacher had varied rubrics so that they matched the student's product if specific directions about what the product might be were not given.

We have chosen to share this example so that teachers will consider carefully the assessment tool that best fits each student product or process.

ADDITIONAL RESOURCES FOR ASSESSMENT

Many Internet sites provide information about student assessment. When this book went to print, they were all active sites. Although sites tend to vanish, new ones are always being developed. For example, the federal government is in the process of selecting regional research sites throughout the United States. When these sites are announced, they probably will have information about literacy assessments.

National Web Sites

http://www.ed.gov. This Web site has information about No Child Left Behind, accountability, and other education issues. It also has research reports and results of international and national studies.

http://www.ed.gov/offices/OERI. This has archived information about educational research and statistics. In 2002 President Bush signed into law the

Education Sciences Reform Act, which produced a new organization, the Institute of Education Sciences (http://www.ed.gov/offices/IES).

http://www.cresst.org. This is the National Center for Research on Evaluation, Standards, and Student Testing. It offers reports, policy briefs, newsletters, and teachers' and parents' pages.

http://www.aera.net. This is the site for the American Educational Research Association. Division D is centered on measurement and research methods, and Division H is centered on school evaluation and program development.

http://www.nationalreadingpanel.org/Publications/researchread.htm. This Web site has the full National Reading Panel report. It also shares other publications such as *Put Reading First: Helping Your Child Learn to Read.*

http://www.edweek.org. EdWeek publishes articles and reports about assessment issues.

Research Centers

Each of the following centers offers research, articles, and monographs about educational issues. Assessment is a common topic.

http://www.ael.org. This is the Appalachian Educational Laboratory. Their specialty is rural education.

http://www.wested.org. This is the Western Educational Laboratory. Their specialty is assessment and accountability.

http://www.ncrel.org. This is the Midwestern Regional Laboratory. Their specialty is technology.

http://www.mcrel.org. This is the Mid-Continent Center for Research on Education and Learning. Their specialty is curriculum, learning, and instruction.

http://www.prel.org. This is the Pacific Resources for Education and Learning. Their specialty is language and cultural diversity.

http://www.nwrel.org. This is the Northwest Regional Educational Laboratory. Their specialty is school change processes.

http://www.alliance.brown.edu. This is the Northeast and Islands Regional Educational Laboratory. Their specialty area is school reform and professional development.

http://www.temple.edu/LSS. This is the Mid-Atlantic Regional Educational Laboratory. Its specialty is urban education.

http://www.serve.org. This is the South Eastern Regional Vision for Education. Its specialty is early childhood education.

http://www.sedl.org. This is the Southwest Educational Development Laboratory (SEDL). Its specialty is language and cultural diversity. SEDL provides a framework of reading assessment. In this framework, links are provided to assessment tools for comprehension, decoding, and so on.

http://www.nwea.org. This organization publishes information on No Child Left Behind, assessment tied to instruction, and other research reports.

http://www2.edtrust.org/edtrust. The Education Trust publishes work related to high academic achievement for all students. They share current federal policies, information for parents, and state and local initiatives.

http://fairtest.org. Fairtest is nationally recognized and at the forefront of assessment reform.

Literacy Organizations

http://www.reading.org. This is the site of the International Reading Association. It offers position statements on high-stakes testing and other topics.

http://www.ncte.org. This is the site of the National Council of Teachers of English. It offers information for teachers, principals, and policymakers about literacy from kindergarten though college.

http://www.nrconline.org. This is the site of the National Reading Conference. It offers literacy research reviews and policy briefs. One brief focuses on high-stakes testing and reading assessment.

Other Sites of Information About Assessment

http://www.literacy.uconn.edu. This site offers information about literacy and links to other literacy sites. It provides information about evaluation.

http://reading.uoregon.edu/assessment/index.php. This site offers information about Reading First, scientific research connected to core reading programs, and information about assessment.

http://www.ciera.org/index.html. This center is no longer operational, but the Web site has information about the improvement of early reading achievement.

http://cela.albany.edu. The National Research Center on English Learning and Achievement provides information related to literacy learning and teaching. Publications focus on assessment and improving student achievement.

http://www.ets.org/research/pic/pir.html. In addition to developing assessments, Educational Testing Service provides policy information and research studies that are targeted to student achievement and assessment. For example, in *Early Literacy Assessment Systems: Essential Elements*, an overview of important concepts related to early literacy and assessment is presented.

http://www.pdkintl.org. Phi Delta Kappa International provides information about schools and teachers. The site has a research section that targets the hottest issues in education.

In this section we have listed selected Web sites with information about literacy assessments. These sites provide a beginning for interested readers. To determine whether the authors of Web sites are reputable and the information provided is current and accurate, look for sites established by national research laboratories created through a rigorous process of selection or by federal or state governments. Also, sites sponsored by national literacy associations provide a wealth of information. Numerous sites established by universities also target literacy and assessment.

FINAL THOUGHTS

Although students are assessed in numerous ways, the most important assessments for instruction are those that teachers routinely conduct with students. Single test scores are certainly the most noticed by those outside a classroom, but it is important to keep them in perspective. A single score is a snapshot: a single, albeit important look at student achievement.

As teachers consider the multiple assessments that are part of instruction, they need to determine how these assessments converge or diverge for single students and classrooms. Often when teachers consider standardized assessments and classroom-based assessments, they get only a single story about a student as high achieving or struggling. However, the data from various assessments often result in a more complex picture. A student may perform well on a classroom assessment in comprehension and struggle with a more formal assessment. In this case, the variation in assessment format could have made the difference. In other cases, it takes more study to better understand how the assessment data represent the strengths and needs of students.

Finally, we share a few ideas about managing and sharing assessment data.

- **Organize data.** Organize class data in a binder for easy reference. Organize each student's data in a folder or section of a binder. Keep student samples to substantiate results from assessments.

- **Include parents and students in assessment.** Parents can offer a view of at-home literacy that informs classroom achievement. Students value and grow from self-assessment. They become partners in establishing personal learning goals.

- **Don't assess everything.** Focus on the most important literacy expectations. It is not necessary to have assessments for minor aspects of the curriculum.

- **Share multiple pieces of data.** When sharing information about a student or class of students, share multiple assessments. For example, share results from a norm-referenced assessment, classroom assessment, and parent and student reflections. Often these conversations are best facilitated by sharing a student's assessment portfolio.

- **Confer with other teachers.** We believe that by working together, teachers can best understand the assessment data they collect. Teachers can target specific worrisome students and plan instruction to enhance learning.

As teachers examine the multiple expectations of assessment and the great variety of assessment materials, it is critical that the end goal—student learning—is always at the forefront. All decisions based on assessments should result in tailored instruction that best meets the needs of students. As teaching is strategically targeted to students, their achievement should be enhanced.

REFERENCES

Cohen, M. (1980). *First grade takes a test.* New York: Dell.

Cooper, J. (1997). *Literacy: Helping children construct meaning.* Boston: Houghton Mifflin.

Hiebert, E., & Calfee, R. (1992). Assessing literacy: From standardized tests to portfolio and performances. In A. E. Farstrup & S. J. Samuels (Eds.), *What research has to say about reading instruction* (2nd ed., pp. 70–100). Newark, DE: International Reading Association.

Linn, R. (2000). Assessment and accountability. *Educational Researcher, 29*(2), 4–16.

Orlofsky, G., & Olson, L. (2001, January 11). The state of the states. *Education Week, 20*(17), 86–108.

Valencia, S. (2002). *Understanding assessment: Putting together the puzzle.* Boston: Houghton Mifflin. Available at http://www.eduplace.com/marketing/nc/author.html

Index